MW00443489

"Of all the moral challenges Christian men face in our culture, sexual temptation is surely one of the most daunting and persistent. Furthermore, this battle has the highest stakes. Thankfully, Fankhauser has given us a terrific road map for developing sexual purity in our sex-saturated culture. This book is exceedingly practical, biblical, and readable. I will be giving *Stormproof Men* to my students, friends, and family members. Put this book on your essential reading list for the year. You will not be disappointed.

—Dr. Steve Tracy, Professor of Theology and Ethics,
Phoenix Seminary; President, Mending the Soul Ministries

Roger Fankhauser has done every Christian man (and many women) a favor by writing a practical book on sexual purity. Through his surveys he knows exactly where Christian men are in their battle against lust. He uses wonderful illustrations and practical examples to show us how solid biblical principles can deliver us from a lifetime of sexual impurity. Needless to say, the wives of the men who use these principles for purity in their lives will be writing thank-you notes to Roger. After all, what wife wants to compete with the internet babes? A must read for any man who wants to be pure.

—Dr. Dave Anderson, President,
Grace School of Theology

Stormproof Men by Dr. Roger Fankhauser can be summed up in a few words. It is biblical, full of wisdom, realistic, relevant, honest and practical. It is a book that was 20 years in the development. What began as a DMin dissertation was honed and helpful to men from the time Roger graduated until the book was finished. Thus, it has been refined by the issues with which Roger has helped men, his own teaching ministry and feedback from men he has helped.

—Dr. John Vawter, Interim Pastor,
Board member of Timothy Connection,
Author of 5 books, conference speaker, church consultant,
Former President, Phoenix Seminary

STORMPROOF MEN

SEXUAL PURITY FOR CHRISTIAN MEN IN A SEX-SATURATED WORLD

ROGER S. FANKHAUSER

Stormproof Men: Sexual Purity for Christian Men in a Sex-Saturated World

Published by Grace Theology Press

The website addresses recommended throughout this book are offered as a resource to you. These websites are not intended in any way to be or imply an endorsement on the part of the author or publisher, nor do we vouch for their content.

Scripture quotations taken from the New American Standard Bible® (NASB), Copyright © 1960, 1962, 1963, 1968, 1971, 1972, 1973, 1975, 1977, 1995 by The Lockman Foundation. Used by permission. www.Lockman.org

ISBN-10: 0-9981385-6-8
ISBN-13: 978-0-9981385-6-5
eISBN-10: 0-9981385-7-6
eISBN-13: 978-0-9981385-7-2

Printed in the United States of America

First Edition 2017

CONTENTS

ACKNOWLEDGEMENTS

All the stories in this book are true, some as compilations of several stories. All the names are changed to protect the identity of the men involved.

Thank you, Dr. Steven Tracy, who started my thinking about sexual purity with a "simple" seminary assignment. After teaching on sexual ethics, he gave this assignment: "Describe the process you would use to help a sex addict." My response started as a very short paper—"I have no clue." I finished the assignment, but it was quite inadequate. This eventually led to my Doctor of Ministry thesis, "Sexual Purity for Non-Sexually Addicted Christian Men." Dr. Tracy served as one of my readers and was a source of encouragement before, during, and after I completed the project.

Thank you, Dr. Fred Chay, the second reader of my dissertation. Dr. Chay encouraged me over the years to "finish my book." It is largely his prompting that resulted in me actually finishing this book!

Thank you to the men of Shreveport Bible Church who encouraged me through attending a couple of versions of teaching this material. Special thanks to David Gilbert who set up the electronic survey used as the research tool for my thesis. And special thanks to Scott Hammond, who encouraged me as I wrote my dissertation, as I developed the teaching material, and as I attempted (unsuccessfully) to master the local golf course.

Thanks, Rich Keller, for your help with the Scripture Index[1] and for fixing the bugs in the tool that my book uncovered!

Thanks to my Burleson Bible Church family for encouraging me to finish this product and supporting me during my sabbatical. This sabbatical allowed me the concentrated time I needed down the stretch to complete the project.

And most important, thanks to my beautiful bride, Debra, who encouraged me to finish this and who put up with my free time being consumed at times during both the dissertation work and my writing this book. She has been my life partner for 42 years as this goes to press. She is the love of my life, and I would not trade our lives together for anything.

Finally, I thank God for the greatness of His grace. He loves us unconditionally, and the free gift of salvation gives the security and safety we need to wrestle with the sins that beset us.

---

1 Scripture index created by Gracelife.org Scripture Indexing Tool, http://gracelife.org/resources/bibletools/, accessed Aug, 20, 2017.

CHAPTER ONE

IN THE MIDST OF THE STORM

You know those balloons that pop up over comic strip characters to show what they are thinking? Imagine sitting in church one Sunday morning and suddenly above the head of every man in the church, one of those balloons appears. And *everyone* can read what is written in them, statements like:

- I masturbate.
- I watch "adult" movies in the motel when I am away on business.
- I love looking at women, especially when I am at the beach.
- I'm married, but I fantasize about what Sue looks like naked and in bed.
- I access internet porn regularly.
- I am having an affair.
- I am attracted to other men.[2]

---

2 The culture widely accepts gender fluidity and same-sex relationships, including same-sex marriage. Addressing either of these topics in depth is beyond the scope of this work. A more specialized work is necessary to address these issues from a biblical perspective. Sexual purity, however, is

These thoughts are just the tip of the iceberg. In our culture, sexual practices run the full gamut, and balloons may pop up with thoughts that run that same gamut. Thoughts which reflect sexual practices less "socially acceptable" than these. And you wonder—no, you are *afraid* of—what your balloon says!

It's a good thing people can't see what we're thinking. Men struggle with sexual purity, and Christians are no exception. In fact, *most* struggle with it on some level! Sometimes, sexual temptation feels like a storm too intense to resist. Chances are good you don't need a description of this storm. In fact, the chances are good that either you or someone close to you is in the midst of the storm and you want some help. Otherwise, why pick up a book about sexual purity?

Before we jump in, let's ask four crucial questions: (1) Do we *want* to experience purity; (2) Is it *possible* to experience purity; (3); What do we think *God* thinks of us; and (4) If it is possible, how in the world do we *experience* purity?

The first question comes from the heart. No book, no counseling, no program can make a person "want to" practice purity or any other biblical principle for that matter. Such tools might help motivate us to want it, or better understand the value of it, but they cannot provide the "want to." Do we want to live as God desires us to live, even in those times when our "want to" is weak? We need to start here. In some way, shape, or form, only if we "want to" will we have any hope of consistently "choosing to." Granted, even if the answer is yes, the "want to" is sometimes derailed by other thoughts, but if the answer to "Do you want to?" is "no," the rest of the story doesn't matter much.

Let me use another issue to clarify this idea. I love to eat, and because I used little self-control in eating, I was overweight. I knew I needed to lose weight, but I did not want to work at it. And so, as time went by, I continued to eat and continued to gain weight. One day, I read Paul's words, "Your body is the temple of the Holy Spirit" and the words

---

independent of these issues. Assuming for the sake of argument that one's orientation is part of his or her nature and thus not a choice, how that person *acts out* is a choice independent of how they perceive their sexuality. To be clear, this book assumes two genders, based on external biology and the biblical description of creation (male and female).

popped into my brain, "And your temple is too big!" I assume the Holy Spirit was applying the Word to my life in this situation. At this point, I had two choices: pursue losing weight or continue ignoring my weight. And then, for the first time in a long time, I *wanted* to get my weight under control. Over the next nine months, I lost over fifty pounds. What changed? I now *wanted* to do what I previously knew I *needed* to do. The temptations still hit me (I love pasta!), but I made different choices than before. Without the "want to" I would not have worked at losing the weight. The same principle applies to sexual purity. For long term success, I must *want* purity. Without this desire, I can only fake it for so long.

So, should you put this book down if the "want to" is not there? Absolutely not! Our "want to" must flow from the heart, but perhaps reading what follows will help change your heart as you see the value of honoring God and experiencing purity. It is fair to start the process because we "need to," but we need to be aware that without the "want to," long-term success may elude us.

This issue leads to another important principle. Is sexual purity primarily a matter of a person's heart or behavior? The answer is, both. The heart addresses our relationship with God, our perspective about sex, our view of sin, and the expectations of real intimacy in relationships vs. the false intimacy offered by sexual impurity. But changing the heart often takes time; it rarely happens in a moment. As we allow God and His Word to work on our heart, we need to make *behavioral* choices that align themselves with purity. If we wait until our hearts are right before making behavioral changes, we will fail. But if we work only on behavior without allowing God to change our heart, we will also fail. Experiencing long-term purity requires a change of heart *and* a change of behavior. Neither is easy, but both are necessary for long-term success. Short term, however, we sometimes must "fake it until we make it" by working on doing right as God works on changing how we think.

That leads logically to another crucial question, which we'll explore more deeply throughout the book, "Is it even *possible* to experience purity?" I may have good intentions, but if I do not believe it is possible, I will still lose the battle. Many times, we feel overwhelmed and overpowered by the temptation. But, God's Word emphatically answers, "Yes you can experience purity!" Paul wrote, "Walk by the Spirit, and you *will not* carry out the desire of the flesh." He doesn't say it will be easy, automatic, or without slip-ups, but the Bible does say "It is possible!"

So, how do I experience it? What do I need to know? What do I need to do? How do I do it? What do I do with my day-to-day thoughts? What do I do when temptation confronts me? That's the purpose of this book: To give biblical and practical tools to help us experience sexual purity.

Do you want to? Only you can answer this. Is it possible? According to God's Word, yes. A third question comes to mind before we can answer the "how to." If we have a wrong answer here, we'll try a wrong approach that addresses the wrong problem. And that question is, what do we think God thinks of us? Notice I did not ask "what *does* God think of us?" but rather, "what do we *think* He thinks?" The answer to these two questions may not be the same.

> What you think about God shapes your whole relationship with him. In addition, what you believe *God* thinks about *you* determines how close you will grow toward him. Many of us have formed a picture of God from impressions we've picked up in passing. If we view him as an overzealous policeman, we'll always be walking on eggshells. If we see him as an angry judge, we'll always feel guilty. If we think he's just like us, we'll be casual about our sin. But are those ideas accurate? What if they're not true at all? Misconceptions about God can create a barrier in your relationship with him. And meanwhile, the friendship, love, and encouragement you could be sharing with your heavenly Father are never realized—all because of wrong conclusions about him.[3]

A man I met admitted he struggled with sexual purity but said he first needed to clean up his life before He could come to God with his problem. I understand how shame can drive a person in this direction;

---

3   Chip Ingram, *God: As He Longs For You to See Him* (Baker Books: Grand Rapids, MI, 2004), 20, emphasis his.

it is logical to feel "I am too dirty to come to God like this." But is this how God sees us, that we need to clean up our lives before we come to Him?

Let's look at five common answers to "what do I think God thinks of me?"

1. God keeps me as his child only if I meet certain performance standards. If I continually sin or lose my faith, I will lose my salvation. With this view, a person believes his position with God is only as secure as his ability to live faithfully. Three consistent results flow from this perspective. First, this person can experience no real security. Anytime they face a sin issue, doubt about their salvation confronts them. Second, once a person believes they have sinned to the point of losing their salvation, the solution becomes getting saved again. However, if they had not learned how to apply the resources God provides for life *before* being re-saved, the problem will likely rear its head again, resulting in a recurring cycle of failure. Third, this kind of thinking fosters wearing masks rather than transparency. We do not want people to know our issues lest they question our salvation.

2. If I continually sin, then I never really believed in the first place. God isn't interested in me, as I am not a "true" believer. I heard someone who struggled with purity conclude this very thing, "Since I cannot gain victory over this sin, I must not really be saved!" The logical results of this view are almost identical to the "I can lose my salvation" view, with one difference. In this view, instead of needing to get re-saved, the person needs to "really believe" and get "really" saved for the first time.[4]

---

4   One well-known theologian sees the similarity of the two views (losing salvation or never saved): "In terms of pastoral care with those who have strayed away from their Christian profession, we should realize that *Calvinists and Arminians . . . will both counsel a 'backslider' in the same way . . .* According to the Calvinist, such a person never really was a Christian in the first place and

3. God is an angry God, focusing on my failures. In the late 1960's, researchers coined the term "the Pygmalion Effect" to describe the phenomenon that teachers' expectations influence student outcomes.[5] In other words, if one teacher saw a group of students as high achievers, the outcome from those students would lean in the direction of higher performance. However, if another teacher saw that same group as low performers, the outcome from those same students would lean towards poorer performance. The "angry God" view sees God in the second group—He sees us as low-performers, needing constant correction. This view often results in focusing too much on failures and divine discipline, leading to a life driven by an unhealthy fear of God.

4. God does not see my sin, as it is all covered by the blood of Christ. This view rightly focuses on my position in Christ and the full forgiveness I experience the moment I believe. However, this view underplays the seriousness of sin and its impact on my ongoing relationship with Christ in our daily lives. It also discounts divine discipline as a consequence of sin in the believer's life.

5. God sees me as His adopted son, recognizes my sin, but encourages me to walk right. He may use divine discipline as an act of love to correct me when necessary, but that is not His usual first response. This view focuses on my position in Christ but also recognizes that God does not ignore my sin.

---

is not one now. But in both cases the biblical counsel given would be the same: 'You do not appear to be a Christian now—you must repent of your sins and trust in Christ for your salvation!'" (Wayne Grudem, *Systematic Theology: An Introduction to Bible Doctrine* [Leicester, England, Grand Rapids, MI: Inter-Varsity Press, Zondervan Publishing House, 2004], 806, emphasis his).

5   http://www.duq.edu/about/centers-and-institutes/center-for-teaching-excellence/teaching-and-learning/pygmalion, accessed Oct. 25, 2015.

I am convinced this last view is the biblical view. At the heart of this view is an understanding of the gospel and what God has done on our behalf when we believe. First, what is required for salvation?

> For I delivered to you as of first importance what I also received, that Christ died for our sins according to the Scriptures . . . and that He was raised on the third day according to the Scriptures. (1 Cor. 15:3-4)

and

> God so loved the world, that He gave His only begotten Son, that whoever believes in Him shall not perish, but have eternal life. (John 3:16)

So, we are saved[6] by just believing in Jesus Christ as the one who died for our sins and was raised from the dead, who gives eternal life to any and all who believe in Him. This initial salvation has no strings attached—that is, our works are not necessary to earn, keep, or prove our salvation. The moment we are saved, God changes our standing before Him forever. In one of the great chapters describing the work of the Trinity regarding our salvation (Ephesians 1:3-14), Paul tells us of

- our adoption as sons through Jesus Christ (1:5)
- our redemption through His blood (1:7)
- the forgiveness of our trespasses (1:7)
- being sealed in Him with the Holy Spirit of promise (1:13)
- the Spirit who is given as a pledge of our inheritance (1:14)[7]

---

6 "Saved" here refers to that moment in time when we receive eternal life or, to use Paul's words, that moment when we are "justified," free (forever) from the penalty of sin.

7 In the recent book, *Position and Condition*, written for "the people in the pew," the author differentiates between our position in Christ and our condition on earth. He rightly defends the position that nothing in my condition (how I live) can ever impact my position, but, if I focus on my position in Christ,

Three times Paul affirms this work of God is done "to the praise of His glory" (1:6, 12, 14). He also asserts God acted "according to the kind intention of His will" (1:5) and "according to the riches of His grace, which he *lavished* on us" (emphasis added). God freely bestowed this grace on us in the Beloved (1:6). And all this happens the moment we believe (1:13). Our salvation is to the glory of God, but it also assures us that He loves us. As such, even His corrective discipline is the act of a loving Father for the good of His children (Heb. 12:4-11). What we think God thinks of us matters because it influences how we *think* He will deal with us in the process of our struggle.

If you do not yet believe the fifth option best describes how He sees you (God sees you as His adopted son, recognizes your sin, but encourages you to walk right), at least be open to seeing God this way. I think as we explore the greatness of His grace and love toward us, you will move towards the view that He treats us out of love—even when He corrects us.

So, finally, we get to the fourth question: How can I experience purity? Keep reading. That's why I wrote this book. However, before we look at the solution, let's first go back in history to see how and where this whole mess started.

The history of both healthy sexuality and sexual sin begins with God's creation of man:

> And God created man in his own image, in the image of God He created him; male and female He created them. (Gen. 1:27)

The Hebrew terms for "male and female" speak of our physical makeup. God created the first two humans as sexual beings, male and female, and every person since then is a sexual being. My maleness is an essential component of my identity:

> Sexuality comprises all aspects of the human person that are related to existence as male and female. Our sexuality, therefore,

---

my condition will improve. This same concept permeates this work. (David R. Anderson, Ph.D., *Position and Condition: An Exposition of the Book of Ephesians*, [NP: Grace Theology Press, 2017]).

is a powerful, deep, and mysterious aspect of our being . . . Our sexuality pervades all our relationships . . . how we think, how we view the world, and how others view us are all affected by our sexuality. We can be human, therefore, only as male or female.[8]

From the beginning, God designed these two sexual beings, male and female, to be attracted to one another.[9] In fact, Adam seems to jump with excitement when he first sees this woman made for him, yet so different than him. It's too easy to read Adam's response to the woman as we might read any book. God had just paraded "every beast of the field and every bird of the sky" before Adam, yet for him "there was not found a helper suitable for him." After Adam had felt this void, God caused him to sleep and then fashioned the woman from his flesh (Gen. 2:19-22). He then brought her to Adam for the first time. Use a little imagination and think about how *you* might feel if you were Adam the very first time this beauty stood before you. I suspect your heart would be racing, adrenaline pumping through your veins, with your eyes open wide in amazement. Try to read these words of Adam with the same enthusiasm: "This is bone of my bone and flesh of my flesh; she shall be called Woman, because she was taken out of man." He might even have yelled, "Wow! Look at her! She is *finally* the one for

---

8   Stanley J. Grenz, *Sexual Ethics: An Evangelical Perspective* (Louisville, KY: Westminster John Knox Press, 1990), 21-22.

9   This book assumes the historical existence of the man Adam and the woman Eve as the first humans, specially created in the image of God. Not all evangelicals hold this view. A movement within evangelicalism, driven in part by its understanding of evolutionary science, believes that there never was a first man named "Adam." One author describes Adam as "a vital, but *incidental*, ancient vessel that transports *inerrant* spiritual truths," that is, Adam did not exist other than as a literary figure to convey certain principles. (Denis O. Lamoureux, "No Historical Adam: Evolutionary Creation View," in Matthew Barrett and Ardel B. Caneday, gen. ed., *Four Views on the Historical Adam* [Grand Rapids, MI: Zondervan, 2013], 37). Despite different interpretative approaches to the creation account, including both young earth and old earth creation views, others affirm the reality of the historical Adam and Eve.

me! This woman is the partner God designed for me! What a beauty!! I am no longer alone!"

From the beginning, God designed these two sexual beings to enjoy sexual intimacy together, to "become one flesh" within the context of marriage *before* sin entered the world (Gen. 2:24). "One flesh" implies real intimacy with the woman in all areas of life, not just the physical relationship, but it certainly *includes* the physical relationship. Adam and his wife were both naked and not ashamed (Gen. 2:24). Nothing interfered with the intimacy these first two humans enjoyed. Neither had any unhealthy views of themselves or any fear of rejection by the other to hinder how they acted and communicated with each other. They had no shame, no internal sense of inadequacy or of feeling unloved. Reading between the lines (since the text doesn't explicitly tell us), they enjoyed a thoroughly satisfying physical relationship with each other because nothing got in the way of their intimacy. I cannot begin to imagine what this true, sinless intimacy was like. God designed sex to be an excellent thing, and the first couple experienced it at its best.

> Sex provides the hope for good far beyond what most people dream or imagine. It can provide physical pleasure, to be sure, but it is also a way of communicating tenderness, compassion, caring, and love. It is a way of showing our most intimate connection with our mates and a way of showing God's intimate communion with us . . . The experience of holy sex is a gift to those who know the One who made it so.[10]

So far, so good; no problems yet. Unfortunately, something drastic happened in chapter three that forever changed humanity. Because of chapter three, my maleness carries another mark from the first two humans. They disobeyed God (they sinned) by eating the fruit of the forbidden tree. Ever since then, every person who has ever lived sins and possesses what the Bible calls "the flesh." The New Testament word

---

10 Tim Alan Gardner, *Sacred Sex* (Colorado Springs, CO: Waterbrook Press, 2002), 19-20.

for flesh (*sarx*) frequently refers to the inner inclination of human beings to sin. This flesh is "regarded as weak and unable to achieve holiness by itself,"[11] and has been "corrupted at its source."[12] And so, every man since then is a sexual being, who is capable of sin, prone to lust and sin.

Becoming a Christian does not exempt us from this propensity to sin. It *does* give us the ability to overcome temptation and sin, but it *does not* eliminate the capacity to sin. Paul writes, "walk by the Spirit, and you will not carry out the desires of the flesh" (Gal. 5:16). Think of the logic here. Why would he write this if a Christian *could not* "carry out the desires of the flesh?" Not surprisingly, he includes sexual sins in the list of the "deeds of the flesh." The first three acts that he records directly address sexual practices: immorality, impurity, and sensuality.[13] The broad term *immorality* means "prostitution, unchastity, fornication, of every kind of unlawful intercourse."[14] It includes adultery (Matt. 19:9), incest (1 Cor. 5:1), same-sex behavior (Jude 7),[15] and intercourse with a prostitute (1 Cor. 6:18). *Impurity* has a wider range of meaning than immorality, referring to "moral uncleanness in thought, word, and deed,"[16] and *sensuality* "connotes an open, shameless, brazen display of these evils."[17] When we pull these three terms together, we see that the flesh produces sexual behavior ranging from impure thoughts to

---

11 John W. Walvoord, s.v., "Flesh" in Don Campbell, et al, *The Theological Wordbook*, (Nashville, TN: Word Publishing, Inc., 2000).

12 F.F. Bruce, *The New International Greek Testament Commentary: The Epistle to the Galatians* (Grand Rapids, MI: William B. Eerdmans Publishing Company, 1982), 247.

13 The Greek terms used here are *porneia*, *akatharsia*, and *aselgeia*.

14 Walter Bauer, *A Greek-English Lexicon of the New Testament*. trans. William F. Arndt, and F. Wilbur Gingrich, 4th ed. (Chicago, IL: University of Chicago Press, 1979), s.v., porneia.

15 Technically, the word here is not *porneia*, but *ekporneuō*, a cognate of *porneia*.

16 Donald K. Campbell, "Galatians," in John F. Walvoord and Roy B. Zuck, *The Bible Knowledge Commentary: An Exposition of Scriptures* (Wheaton, IL: Victor Books, 1983), 607.

17 Ibid., 607.

all kinds of overt sexual acts—and every one of these behaviors are contrary to God's design for sex. We are fully capable of thinking about or doing any of them.

The problem is not sex itself:

> But untold millions have also been devastated and even destroyed, either emotionally or physically through the evils of sex. This evil that is associated with sex comes from the *abuse* of God's gift, not from the gift itself. God intended sex to be loving and pleasurable, not a source of heartache and destruction.[18]

We live in a sex-saturated world that flaunts the abuse of God's gift. Sexual images and messages bombard us. Sometimes, they come our way unexpectedly and without invitation. Some years ago, I was traveling overseas and had a layover in Amsterdam. The sexual mores in Amsterdam are far more liberal than in my home state, but I was tired from traveling and didn't think much about those differences. To stay awake while waiting for my next flight, I decided to visit a bookstore in the airport. As I wandered the aisles, I came to one filled with sexually explicit books and magazines. I wasn't looking for them—they came uninvited (I quickly left the store, by the way).

On another day, I attended a college homecoming football game with a friend. Little did I know that the closest parking spot required a long walk by myself across campus, walking past hundreds of tailgating students. Some of the young women were clothed immodestly, some to the point of being provocative. Such "eye candy" provided ample temptation for wandering eyes and wandering thoughts to move into dangerous territory. I wasn't looking for women clothed this way; they just happened to be along the route I needed to take.

These examples seem mild in the world of sexual temptation. Some men face deeper temptations, like the allure of the strip club or the pull of the "adult" bookstore that they pass driving down the freeway.

---

18 Gardner, 19-20, emphasis added.

Sexual messages and images bombard us, often uninvited. Too many times, however, we *intentionally* pursue sexual stimulation. Instead of *being* tempted, we *pursue* temptation.

One such far-too-common pursuit is the anonymity of internet pornography. I recently searched the internet using the word "sex," and the search engine located almost 3.5 *billion* web pages.[19] How big is this number? If someone spent an average of 60 seconds per page, 24 hours per day, 7 days per week nonstop until he looked at every page (taking no time for sleep, food, or anything else), he would be online for over 6,500 years! Christian men pursue cyber-sex; they are not immune to its allure. The leader of a ministry at a major university told me that virtually *every* male student he works with wrestles with porn to some degree. And, in a survey of Christian men, over half who responded said they *intentionally* accessed internet pornography during the previous year.[20]

Viewing pornography almost always leads to masturbation. I'll address the issue of masturbation in Chapter Four but for now, for the sake of argument, assume it is outside of God's design for healthy sex. Men commonly practice masturbation, even Christian men. In the same survey, seven out of ten men admitted they masturbate at least once per month. The average frequency was six times per month, and many reported masturbating more than ten times per month! But that's not all. Christian men fantasize, have inappropriate sexual thoughts, allow their eyes to travel where they know they should not go and engage in all kinds of sexual behavior. Being a Christian does not exempt us from sexual temptations.

Sometimes, ordinary life experiences intensify the appeal to yield to sexual temptation. Consider, for example, a happily married man. Typically, men desire sex more frequently than women (at this point, I can hear many readers saying, "Well, duh!"). When Christian men and women were asked how often their thoughts turned to sex, 70 percent

---

19 www.google.com, accessed November 11, 2016.

20 Roger S. Fankhauser, "Sexual Purity for Non-Sexually Addicted Christian Men," (unpublished Doctor of Ministry Dissertation, Phoenix Seminary, 2006), hereafter, "my survey."

of women said once per week or *less*, but almost 80 percent of men said once per day or *more!*[21]

How Often Our Thoughts Turn to Sex

Frequency	Men	Women
Once per month or less	5%	27%
Weekly	17%	43%
Daily	61%	28%
Once an hour or more	17%	2%

Frustrations from these differences often rise to the surface in a marriage. "I don't understand why my wife isn't interested in sex a couple of times per day," lamented one married man. "Why did God make us *so* different?" asked another. Men sometimes use this difference to justify their sexual conduct (aka, sin): "I just need a release, and this respects my wife's different desires."

Sometimes, men try to use the Bible to their advantage. By applying a little biblical pressure to his wife, this man hopes to convince her that she should have sex as frequently as *he* desires. "The woman does not have authority over her own body but the *husband* does," he quotes.[22] Of course, he fails to apply the second half of the verse: "And likewise

---

21 The absolute numbers are less important than the trend: Men, as a group, desire sex or think about sex more frequently than women. The results of a cursory internet search for statistics on the frequency of sexual desire confirm this conclusion, whether reporting scholarly articles or anecdotal data. The data for men reported here are from Dr. Archibald D. Hart, *The Sexual Man: Masculinity Without Guilt* (Dallas: Word Publishing, 1994), 58; data for women are from Archibald D. Hart, Ph.D., Catherine Hart Weber, Ph.D., and Debra L. Taylor, M.A., *Secrets of Eve: Understanding the Mystery of Female Sexuality* (Nashville, TN: Word Publishing, 1998), 63. These data describe statistical trends; individual interest levels may vary. In some cases, the wife is interested in sex more often than the husband.

22 1 Cor. 7:4

also the husband does not have authority over his own body, but the *wife* does." Think of what happens when both partners selfishly try to force their application of this passage on their spouse. The man, typically interested in sex more often the woman, might say, "Every day! Your body is mine, and I want sex every day. The Bible says so!" The woman, less interested in sex, and worn out from raising the children at home, responds, "Maybe once a year. Your body is mine, and I am just fine without sex. Once a year is just fine with me. The Bible says so!" If *either or both* use the passage selfishly, *neither* will be content. The passage only works when each partner views their physical relationship through a servant's heart. The man who tries to manipulate his wife with this verse most often finds himself *more* frustrated than before!

Single men, on the other hand, face a different scenario. Their frustration stems from living in a sex-saturated world *without* the biblical option of a sexual relationship within marriage. However, between pornography and all-too-rampant pre-marital sex,[23] he has opportunities (albeit sinful ones) for sexual expression outside of the marriage bed. The scenario he faces differs from the married man, but his struggle is just as real. He may justify his sexual conduct (aka, sin): "I just need a release, but I have no wife, so long-term, this reduces my lust."

Feel the frustration? The believer faces another issue which the unbeliever does not face: Despite the sexual frustrations he faces; despite the ease of access to explicit material; despite any frustrations he may experience within marriage; despite the sexual pressure he may face as a single man, the believer *still* stands under God's unchanging standard. Even in this fallen, sexually charged world, God *still* commands us to "flee immorality."

So let's go back to the original question: How and where did this mess start? How did men get into this genuine and very intense

---

23 The data from one survey shows that only 6% of never-married women between the ages of 18 and 23 and in a dating relationship are *not* having sex. (Mark Regnerus and Jeremy Uecker, *Premarital Sex in America: How Young Americans Meet, Mate, and Think About Marrying* [New York: Oxford Press, 2011], 16.)

struggle? The answer: God designed us as sexual beings, who, after the fall, are fully capable of sinning (because of the flesh), who now live in a fallen, sex-saturated culture where sexual temptations inundate us. And this same God commands purity even in this messy world.

Sadly, however, we feel stuck. We know we are supposed to flee, but we do not know *how*. We yield to sexual temptation, perhaps "innocently" watching the woman walking by, perhaps something more. We are not sure how to stop. In fact, we may feel we are powerless to stop. Is there any *real* hope to withstand the storm of sexual temptation?

Sometimes, men turn to other believers—including leaders—for help. Sometimes, they give helpful advice. Sometimes, to be honest, the advice is bad, albeit well-intentioned. "I have a hard time controlling my impure thoughts, and I wind up masturbating. What should I do?" asked Brian of Bob, a mature man in his church. Bob told Brian to stop. Nothing else. Brian *knew* he needed to stop; what he wanted was some help figuring out *how* to stop. Instead, he walked away feeling disappointed, guilty, and even more frustrated. Steve received different advice when he asked a pastor on staff at his church about the same issue. The pastor advised him that the Bible didn't directly discuss masturbation, so he was not forbidden to practice it. However, Steve knew he had a problem. He couldn't seem to control his desire to masturbate, and he was frustrated he could not get help within his church.

If this were the entire story, we'd likely give up. Sexual temptation is powerful; most men struggle with it; the Bible sets a seemingly impossible goal of avoiding any and all sexual sin, and other Christians are sometimes unhelpful.

There *is* hope! My intention for this book is to help us become "stormproof men," to provide tools to help withstand sexual temptations. Before looking at the specifics, though, we need to look at the "big picture" of where the book is headed.

When I began thinking about the topic of sexual purity, I thought "fleeing immorality" was *the* key biblical principle to apply. As crucial as this principle may be, I now believe the Bible provides *many* principles that apply to our purity, and "fleeing" is the last step. When a man discovers and practices some the other principles of Scripture, he finds less need to "flee" because he finds himself in harm's way less frequently.

Paul gives us one of the "big picture" passages that deal with overcoming temptation in 1 Cor. 10:13. He wanted his readers to learn from the mistakes made by Israel (1 Cor. 10:6, 10, 12). He reminded his readers of the man caught in the act of sex with a Moabite woman, both of whom were put to death mid-act (Num. 25:1-9). With this event in mind, he challenged his readers—and us—to "not act immorally as some of them did." Israel failed, but Paul did not want his readers to fail. He summarized with four key principles regarding temptation in 1 Cor. 10:13:

No temptation has overtaken you but such as is common to man; and God is faithful, who will not allow you to be tempted beyond what you are able, but with the temptation will provide a way of escape also, so that you may be able to endure it.

1. No one's struggles are unique. Humanity has struggled with immorality for ages. Some of the specific forms vary (after all, I don't think the internet was a problem in Paul's day), but sexual temptations are not new. And they are not unique—other men struggle with the same issues with which each of us struggles, no matter how severe those problems may be. Too many hide their struggles from others and feel like they are the only ones facing this particular temptation. In this frame of mind, they certainly will not want to admit to someone that they need help. But, their struggles are normal! "Normal" does not mean their actions are right, only that the problems are not unique and that *no person is alone* in their struggle. Paul counters the lie many believe, "You are the only one who sins like this. You are hopeless."

2. We do not find the keys to victory through self-effort. Instead, they lie in the person and work of God. Paul here simply says, "God is faithful." Both the *means* and the *power* for enduring the temptation come from God. This short statement gives us a glimpse into the greatness of God and His provisions on our behalf.

3. As strong as sexual temptation may feel, that strength pales in comparison to the power of God. He will not allow us to be tempted or tested beyond what we can endure. We might *think* it is more than we can endure, but *thinking* it is more is different than it *being* more than we can endure.

4. The faithful God promises to provide a way of escape so that the believer can withstand the temptation or test. Walt once told me about his struggle with drug addiction. He said he repeatedly prayed that God would remove the temptation from him (a legitimate request), but the temptation did not go away. Asking God to remove the temptation falls short of what God promised. He *may* remove the temptation, but He does not *promise* to remove it. God promises a "way of escape," a way out, a way of success. Unfortunately, Walt yielded to his temptation and fell back into drug use. Perhaps his battle would have turned out differently had he instead looked for the "way of escape." The principle holds true for anyone trying to live a sexually pure life. God never promises to remove sources of sexual temptation. If he did, much of the world would grind to a screeching halt! He would have to eliminate all women from around us, erase memories from our minds, and reprogram how we think. That's not going to happen! Regardless, He does promise a "way of escape." So, a better prayer would ask Him to show the way of escape and to give the wisdom and strength to *use* that escape route!

Since Scripture is true, *since* God is faithful, and *since* God promised He would not allow us to be tempted beyond what we can endure, we have real hope for success and real help from Him. The purpose of this book is to help discover that hope and help. We *can* experience purity before the sexual struggle engulfs us.

As you read on, keep four thoughts in mind. First, this book is designed for all men, including the married man who enjoys a normally-satisfying sex life with his wife, the married man with a less-than-satisfying sex life with his wife, and the unmarried man with no marriage bed in his life.

Second, merely reading the book is not enough. A young man recently came to me and bluntly told me he needed help controlling his sexual behavior. He was accessing internet pornography, and he knew he shouldn't do so. He said he had read all the books, but still struggled. He knew what different authors said, but he didn't know how to apply what they said to his life. His experience reminds us that *knowing* what to do is not enough. Reading is helpful, but we must apply (and apply and apply) what we learn if we want success.

Third, keep in mind the "want to" factor. Knowing what to do and how to do it loses its potency when the "want to" is gone. Here's the simple truth: Any time we face a sexual temptation, if we don't "want to" experience purity, we set ourselves up to fail. Do I "want to" do what is right, what honors God, or do I "want to" give in to the sexual temptation? I hope as you work through the biblical truths in this book, your "want to" will grow stronger.

Fourth, the battle is not a one-time-wins-all battle. It only takes a few days to read a book or a few hours to learn some principles, but we must live out those principles over a lifetime. In one of his discourses about discipleship, Jesus told the disciples to take up their crosses *daily* (Luke 9:23). The principle certainly applies in the area of sexual purity. Sexual messages bombard us daily; access to sources of (false) satisfaction is but one website away. The battle never ceases, but neither does God's faithfulness. Some days we may not feel like enduring the battle, but don't give up. Keep applying the principles. The battle may never become easy, but it can become easier!

The approach this book takes parallels the structure of a home. My wife and I bought the house we now live in as it was being built. All that we had on the lot at the time was the foundation. Soon, we watched them build the frame. We didn't think about it much at the time, but both the foundation and the frame had to be strong for the house to last. With a bad foundation or with the wrong materials or with poor construction of the frame, what is now a lovely home would instead be a disaster. It would not stand up to the normal wear-and-tear of life, let alone withstand any storms that came our way. We wanted a house like that in Jesus' words:

Therefore everyone who hears these words of Mine and acts on them, may be compared to a wise man who built his house on the rock. And the rain fell, and the floods came, and the winds blew and slammed against that house; and *yet* it did not fall, for it had been founded on the rock. (Matt. 7:24-25)

Picture healthy sexual expression—purity—as the home itself. Five key principles (connect regularly with God, involve others, control your thoughts, control your eyes, and flee), form the frame of this home which we build on the foundation of God's person, power, and provisions. Too often, we try to build this home without an adequate foundation or the right frame. And then, when storms hit (temptations), the structure crumbles. Jesus talked about this kind of poorly-built house—a house built on sand (the wrong foundation) which crumbled:

Everyone who hears these words of Mine and does not act on them, will be like a foolish man who built his house on the sand. The rain fell, and the floods came, and the winds blew and slammed against that house; and it fell—and great was its fall." (Matt. 7:26-27)

When we build this home of our healthy sexuality on the right foundation with the right frame, we can stand up to the storms that hit. We can be "stormproof men." Such men have:

- A healthy view of God
- A healthy view of their identity in Christ
- A healthy view of the seriousness of sin
- A healthy awareness of their weaknesses
- An awareness of the temptations that most affect them
- A good definition of sexual purity
- Healthy relationships with others who can encourage and challenge them
- A healthy view of women

- A healthy spiritual walk
- A process for evaluating and changing their thought life
- A process to control their eyes
- The presence of mind to fight temptations when they strike

So, are you ready to begin the process? Let's start by figuring what we mean by "sexual purity." The answer may not be as obvious as you think!!

CHAPTER TWO

WHAT IS OUR TARGET?

What is your goal in the battle with sexual temptation?
This may seem like a silly question. We don't want the temptation to overpower us, right? The question is not that simple, though, because the answer will dictate, to a large degree, how successful we will be in the battle. Think of these four possible responses:

- I want to quit feeling guilty.
- I want God to remove the temptation.
- I want to say "no" to the temptation.
- I want to honor God.

Before reading on, take a few minutes and choose the option you desire for yourself. Don't automatically select the "church" answer!

Okay, now that you have made a choice, let's look at each option more carefully.

The first option is easy to address. If we want the guilt to go away, then it seems we aren't striving for sexual purity. We simply do not want to feel bad because of our actions. Imagine, for example, accessing the website "woo_hoo_hoo_xxx.com" (a fictional domain name at the time of this writing). You spend too much time perusing the porn and then masturbate to the images on your screen. Later, you remember the principle, "flee immorality" and you feel guilty, a valid guilt because you failed to obey the Scriptures. You did not flee immorality; you chased it.

True guilt (that is, the awareness that we have sinned) comes when we have done something wrong, and we know we have done something wrong.[24] Negative emotions such as sadness or embarrassment may accompany this guilt.[25] For the believer, guilt arises because of the work of our conscience, of the Holy Spirit within us, and of the Word of God. If the only thing we desire is for this guilt to go away—a legitimate awareness that we sinned—then we are focused on how we *feel* about our thoughts or actions rather than the *rightness* of them. The Bible calls this "hardening of our heart" or "searing of our conscience."

Desiring our guilt to go away is much like wanting the red warning light on the car dashboard to go away. When the red light says "Service Engine Soon," the problem is not the red light! Something in my engine needs attention, and the warning light lets me know about it so I can address the problem. True guilt serves a similar purpose. Just as the red light on the dashboard indicates something in our car is in need of repair, guilt warns us something in our lives is in need of repair. The solution is not "disconnect the light," but rather "fix the problem." Eliminating guilt does not address sexual purity.

Many choose the second option: I want God to remove the temptation. But this goal often leaves us frustrated. Some sources of

---

24 Some may object to the term "guilt" since it is not used in the New Testament anywhere outside the gospels. For purposes of this book, "guilt" refers to the primary dictionary definition, "the fact of having committed a breach of conduct . . ." but, unlike the dictionary definition, it excludes "feelings of culpability especially for imagined offenses or from a sense of inadequacy." (*Merriam-Webster's Collegiate Dictionary, 11th Edition,* [Springfield, MA: Merriam-Webster, Inc., 2003], s.v. "guilt."). It is a recognition that one has sinned.

25 Such negative emotions may accompany both guilt and shame. It is not the emotions that distinguish the two but rather the thoughts that accompany them. We discuss shame more fully in Chapter Five and guilt in Chapter Eleven.

temptation are completely out of our control and if we ask God to remove the temptation, we want Him to change the world around us to make life easier for us. Of course, when this does not happen, we could respond by being disappointed or frustrated that God didn't rescue us. Notice the selfishness in this? God needs to orchestrate *my* world so that I am not tempted.

As we saw in Chapter One, God *never* promises to remove temptations. Some years ago, I was in a casual conversation with a Christian man who said he knew his smoking was a sin. He rationalized that God had not yet removed the temptation from him, so he continued to smoke. The point is not whether smoking is sinful, but rather how this man justified his actions. God did not remove the temptation, so he thought he was excused. But, we're setting ourselves up for failure if we believe that God must do something He never promised (i.e., remove the temptation).

Asking God to remove the temptation is a valid prayer. The problem arises when we *expect* God to remove the temptations as if He promised to do so. He did promise a way of escape (1 Cor. 10:13), but He never promised to eliminate them. So, if your goal is "I want God to remove the temptation," you'll likely be frustrated.

The third option seems like a great one: I want to say "no" when tempted. Fleeing sexual immorality, of course, includes saying "no" to sexual temptation. If I think about logging into an inappropriate website, or if I allow my eyes to linger where they should not be lingering, or if I think about acting out in any way that is unbiblical, I need to say "no." I need to recognize temptation when it comes (and trust me, it *will* come!) and then refuse to yield to it.

No doubt this is a great goal, but it, too, falls short. This goal is measured only by what we do *not* do, "I am sexually pure if I say no to inappropriate sexual activity." Negative statements such as "say no" may initially motivate change, but many times they frustrate. Negatives can start us in the right direction but rarely sustain positive movement forward. I remember when my children were little and (seemingly) always getting into things, my conversation with them seemed to consist of only three words: "Don't . . . stop . . . quit." I felt frustrated since it seemed I was always emphasizing the negative. The negative demands were necessary (after all, what father *wants* his child to eat crickets?). But, over the long haul, we also need something positive to replace the negative. For my kids, I needed something like "Stop running in the house. Instead, go outside and run around the back yard!" In the same way, I need my goal for purity to include more positive motivators than just the negative "don't do this."

You've probably guessed by now that I believe the best goal in our battle for sexual purity is the positive goal of honoring God. When we look carefully at the Bible, we find God balances "thou shalt not" with "thou shalt." He gives positive commands that we ought to follow as we give up whatever is prohibited. The consistent pattern is "Don't do this. Do this instead." Sometimes, the "do this instead" is found in the greater context, but it is there. Here are a few examples:

Prohibition ("Don't do this"): "You shall have no other gods before me." (Ex. 20:3)

Positive principle ("Do this instead"): "I am the Lord your God who brought you out of the land of Egypt," Paraphrased, "Have *Me* as the God before you." (Ex. 20:2).

Prohibition: "Be anxious for nothing" (Phil. 4:6a).

Positive principle: "But in everything by prayer and supplication with thanksgiving let your request is made known to God" (Phil. 4:6b).

Prohibition: "Let us lay aside every encumbrance and the sin that so easily entangles us" (Heb. 12:1b).

Positive principle: "Fixing our eyes on Jesus, the author and perfecter of faith" (Heb. 12:2a).

Get the idea? Here is a set that directly addresses purity:

Prohibition: "Flee immorality" (1 Cor. 6:18a).

Positive principle: "Glorify God in your body" (1 Cor. 6:20).

A short definition of sexual purity is, "*Glorifying God by applying biblical principles regarding my sexual practices.*" Based on the clear biblical charge to glorify God in our body (the goal of purity), it makes biblical sense to include both the prohibitions (what to avoid) and the positive principles (what to do instead) in describing what purity looks like:

I experience purity to the degree that I make godly choices

- *by avoiding all inappropriate sexual activity*
- *by enjoying appropriate expressions of masculinity*
- *by enjoying appropriate relations with the opposite sex*
- *that glorify God*
- *that respect me*
- *that honor others*
- *that I act on with my heart, mind, eyes, and actions*

In this full description, we see one prohibition, five positive principles, and a description of the breadth of the principles. Admittedly, it looks impossible to achieve (and it is, on our own. More will be said later about the "power source" necessary to implement them in our lives). For now, keep reading to understand this description better. We will look at the seemingly strange condition "to the degree that" after exploring the rest of the description.

In the prohibition "avoiding all inappropriate sexual activity" we need to define "sexual activity." For our purposes, sexual activity comes under two categories. The first covers any sexual activity that, taken to its natural conclusion, results in orgasm. So, sexual intercourse fits the definition. But so does oral sex and anal sex and caressing sexual organs (breasts and genitals), whether unclothed, under clothing, or through clothing and masturbation and maybe "passionate" kissing, the kind that ignites sexual arousal.[26] The umbrella of sexual activity—

---

26 Why does "passionate kissing" fall under the umbrella of "sexual activity?" Some kisses show appropriate affection between two people. But some kissing ignites the physical passion that may well lead to other sexual activity. The

which pertains to our purity—covers a much wider range of activities than just intercourse. Achievement of orgasm is not *necessary* for some action to fit the definition of "sexual activity." However, if orgasm would occur if we carry the activity to culmination, then it comes under the umbrella.

The second category of sexual activity includes "hypothetical" actions linked with our eyes and thoughts. Engaging in sexual fantasy, recalling sexual memories, anticipating a sexual experience, thinking "I would if I could" about someone, eyeing a woman's figure (regardless of how much skin is showing), all fall under the umbrella of sexual activity—even though nothing happens that is overtly sexual. Other voyeuristic practices fall under this second category, such as being a "peeping Tom," looking at internet pornography, sexting, reading sex stories, and even intentionally watching movies or television shows for sexual content. As Jesus put it, "Everyone who *looks* at a woman with lust for her has already committed adultery with her *in his heart*" (Matt. 5:28, emphasis added).

Sexual activity covers a wide range of practices.

This broad understanding of sexual activity is crucial. We saw in Chapter One that the sexual deeds of the flesh (immorality, impurity, and sensuality) describe many more activities and thoughts than just vaginal intercourse. However, many people today are not clear about what they believe constitutes sex. They certainly identify intercourse as "sex" but not necessarily other sexual activities. In a study published in 2010, respondents were asked, "Would you say you 'had sex' with someone if the most intimate behavior you engaged in was...", followed by specific situations.[27] Not surprisingly, almost all agreed that penile-vaginal intercourse was sex. But a lower number agreed

---

kissing itself does not result in orgasm, but under the right circumstances, it may well lead to activity that would.

27 Stephanie A. Sanders, et al., "Misclassification bias: diversity in conceptualis-ations [*sic*] about having 'had sex,'" *Sexual Health*, 2010, 7, 31-34. The survey included 14 different situations, but all are variations of the four categories listed in the table. The purpose of the study was to determine the need for behavior-specific terminology in research and clinical practice involving sex or in taking of sexual histories.

that penile-anal intercourse or oral contact was sex, and less than half said that manual stimulation of genitals was sex. A significantly lower percentage of respondents under 30, and especially men under 30, said oral contact or manual stimulation was sex.

Would you say you had sex with someone if the most intimate behavior was:	Percentage who said yes	
	Overall	Ages 18-29 only
Partner touched, fondled, or manually stimulated your genitals	48.1	16.7 (men), 32.3 (women)
Partner had oral contact with your genitals	72.9	40.0 (men), 67.7 (women)
Penile-Anal intercourse	80.8	76.7 (men), 83.9 (women)
Penile-Vaginal intercourse	94.8	96.7 (men), 93.5 (women)

The survey did not ask if they considered these actions sexual *activity*, but the results do show how the culture understands "having had sex." Each of these behaviors falls under the umbrella of sexual activity. This leads to the logical question: how do we distinguish between appropriate sexual activity and inappropriate activity? Our response must reflect a biblical worldview, not a cultural worldview such as that revealed in the above survey.

And the answer is: "Appropriate sexual activity" depends on the relationship. "Appropriate" for husband and wife differs from "appropriate" for any other relationship. Our culture mostly believes that boundaries about appropriateness are not good, and sometimes our sexual desires make us question whether or not they are good.

Let's first look at sex within marriage. Almost anything a husband and wife choose to do sexually is appropriate. The Scripture teaches that sex between husband and wife should be great! The biblical books, Song of Solomon, Proverbs, and Hebrews, all proclaim the goodness of marital sex. When I was in seminary, we were required to learn the basic theme of each book of the Bible. My professor gave us this theme for the strongly sexual book, The Song of Solomon: "Wowie Zowie!" The thrust of Scripture teaches that within the marriage relationship, the husband and wife can enjoy sexual "wowie zowie" as an expression of intimacy, as one dimension of the "one flesh" relationship in God's design for marriage. Such sexual expression provides the real intimacy and fulfillment that inappropriate sexual activity promises but cannot deliver.

Keep in mind that intimacy involves more than sex (sorry, guys!). Many men (maybe most men) think like this when they hear the word "intimacy":

Intimacy = Sexual pleasure

However, this definition fits neither the biblical idea nor what most women think when *they* hear the word! When we limit intimacy to sexual pleasure, we miss a crucial dimension of the relationship we may enjoy with women. When women think of intimacy, the definition often looks something like this:

Intimacy = A connection of hearts, physical and emotional closeness, spending time together, talking, being romantic, being appreciated for more than sex.

Men often use sex to express, and even feel, the emotions of love and affection . . . Women, on the other hand, want to talk, touch, and feel love, then (maybe) express it by having sex. This difference in priority is evident in how low on their list 'making love' is as their preference for expressing love to their partner: Less than one-third (28%) chose 'making love' and 22% chose 'going out for a romantic evening.' And remember, to a woman a romantic evening may or may not include sex.[28]

---

28 Hart, Weber, and Taylor, 44.

Thus, most women view intimacy more broadly than just the physical act of sex. This view better fits the biblical concept of one-flesh intimacy. Real biblical intimacy requires connecting on many levels, including spiritual and emotional closeness as well physical closeness. The biblical commands given to the husband reflect this broad understanding of intimacy, commands to love his wife as Christ loved the church, to live with her in an understanding way, and to honor her as a fellow-heir,[29] True intimacy involves much more than sexual activity. In fact, we can enjoy spiritual and emotional intimacy *without* sexual activity!

Nonetheless, God did design "wowie zowie" as one dimension of the "one flesh" relationship husbands and wives should enjoy together. However, even this design has boundaries for what is and is not appropriate. I see three such boundaries. First, when we understand God's design for sex as mutual enjoyment which honors one another, we can exclude unhealthy or hurtful practices as inappropriate. Any masochistic or sadistic sex violates the idea of honoring our bodies and honoring our partner and therefore falls outside the bounds of appropriate sex. I would also put anal sex in this category because of the health risks involved,[30] because the anus is not designed for penile penetration, and because women generally do not enjoy it:

> Anal sex largely lacks mutual pleasure for most, at least from what interviewees told us when we asked them about it. And it implies physical risks—since the anal wall is thinner and less lubricated than the vagina—as well as the 'ick' factor for many . . . Only 15 percent of never-married women ages 18-23 . . . who had ever had anal sex with their current partner reported liking it 'very much,' down from 38 percent who said the same thing about performing oral sex and 83 percent who said that about vaginal sex.[31]

---

29 Eph. 5:25, 1 Pet. 3:7a, I Pet. 3:7b.

30 www.webmd.com/sex/anal-sex-health-concerns#1, accessed August 4, 2017.

31 Regnerus and Uecker, 86.

Second, neither partner should try to make the other do something they feel uncomfortable doing, even if it is not, in itself, inappropriate. This boundary differs for each couple, and it might even change at different stages of the relationship. Since I don't want to create too many sexual images in the book, let me use a silly example (after all, it seems counter-productive to write a book about sexual purity which includes provocative stories or illustrations!). Let's say you love to hold hands in public. Your wife, however, does not like to hold hands in public. At some time in your relationship, you talked about it, and your wife told you she disliked it. Today the two of you are enjoying a day at the zoo, and you reach for her hand. But you remember she doesn't like holding hands in public. What should you do? You could either pull your hand back or even ask permission to hold it. But if she says "no" and you take her hand anyway, you have violated a boundary. You have now turned the expression from something mutually enjoyable into a selfish act, one that does not honor her. Granted, this is a silly illustration, but I think you get the point. If your partner is uncomfortable doing something that is otherwise permissible, honor the boundary and, in so doing, honor her.

The third boundary sounds odd. The third boundary addresses how we think about our spouse. I firmly believe I can enjoy thoughts of past experiences with my wife, and thoughts of future time together. So what boundaries should I have for my thought life about *my* wife? I need to guard against objectifying her—thinking of her as a body for my pleasure. Instead, I need to think of her as a whole person. And, I need to guard against fantasies with her involving activities in which she does not wish to participate. In my mind, I need to avoid making her into somebody that she is not.

With these three boundaries in mind—avoiding unhealthy or hurtful activities, avoiding those actions that make her uncomfortable, and avoiding thinking about her in an unhealthy way, we are free to enjoy one another thoroughly! Husband and wife have great freedom in their sexual relationship. If you wish to explore legitimate ways to enhance your sex life, log on to a Christian bookstore or book distributor (not a secular source—who knows what you will find there!) and search using "sexual fulfillment" or "marital sex." Find a book or other resource, read it together, have fun, and grow in your relationship together![32]

The first principle in experiencing purity—the prohibition—defines what we should avoid: all inappropriate sex. The next five positive principles describe what we should do instead: The first two, *enjoying appropriate expressions of masculinity*[33] and *enjoying appropriate relations with the opposite sex,* overlap, so we'll look at them together.

My sexuality is part of who I am. Every man, no matter his marital status, can enjoy appropriate expressions of his masculinity. I can do "man things" with other men (or by myself) such as fishing, hunting, golfing, watching baseball, riding a motorcycle, channel surfing, working with power tools, cutting down trees or a host of other such typical acts. However, we can enjoy other activities thought by some to be less "masculine." I, for example, enjoy watching "Project Runway" or some "chick-flicks" with my wife. Experiencing purity does not mean I stop being a "manly man," rather, it means I can still enjoy being who I am as God created me.

In the context of enjoying appropriate masculinity, what does "enjoying appropriate relationships with the opposite sex" look like? It looks much different for the married man and his wife than for the same man with a different woman. We have crossed the line when we have sexual contact with another woman. Intercourse with my wife is appropriate; intercourse with my neighbor's wife is not. Kissing my wife is appropriate; kissing my neighbor's wife is not. You get the idea! We have also crossed the line when we move beyond simply noticing another woman's attractiveness and instead focus on body parts or begin to think thoughts like "If I could, I would. . . ." We've also crossed the line when we engage in inappropriate conversation. A safe question to help determine if our words or actions are appropriate as a married

---

32 For example, Clifford & Joyce Penner, *The Gift of Sex: A Guide to Sexual Fulfillment* (Nashville, TN: Thomas Nelson, 2003).

33 Keep in mind that over the years, culture has defined and redefined what is and isn't masculine or feminine. The point here is not to be masculine as defined by culture. Much of the culture today accepts gender fluidity, a topic beyond the scope of this work. See footnote 2, chapter 1.

man is, "What would my wife think if I _____ (fill in the blank with the words or actions)."

What about the unmarried man? What is appropriate for him? He is free to enjoy some physical contact with a woman (holding hands, hugs, appropriate kissing), spending time with her, enjoying conversations with her, and the like. But regarding sexual activity, the message is "Wait!"[34] Practice abstinence until marriage. I know our culture pushes a different message. It says casual sex, sex outside of marriage, cohabitation, oral sex when dating, pornography and the like are normal and acceptable. Our culture does not promote the message "wait." And so, many Christian men and women do not practice waiting. In my survey of Christian men, almost 90% of the single men who responded said they masturbate on some frequency, averaging about twice per week (nearly twice that of non-singles). Over 40% of singles reported they have sex such as intercourse, oral sex, or masturbation with a partner at least "sometimes."

The third positive principle in the description of purity, *choices that glorify God*, recognizes our "higher calling" to God as believers. Our lives should be characterized as God-centered, not me-centered. The themes of the glory of God and glorifying Him fill the pages of Scriptures. For example,

> Flee immorality. Every other sin that a man commits is outside the body, but the immoral man sins against his own body. Or do you not know that your body is a temple of the Holy Spirit who is in you, whom you have from God, and that you are not your own? For you have been bought with a price: therefore *glorify God* in your body. (1 Cor. 6:18-20, emphasis added)

To glorify God simply means we bestow honor and praise on Him (to "put the spotlight" on God). The better we understand who He is, what

---

34 "Wait" seems a better response than "Don't," although functionally they look alike. The message "wait" recognizes the value of delayed gratification, that celibacy is good (even though frustrating at times), and that the single person may one day marry, at which point sexual activity is not only appropriate but encouraged.

He has done for us, and who we are in Him, the greater will be our desire to glorify Him. In this passage alone, we see that He has given us the Holy Spirit, that we are His temple, and that we belong to Him because we have been "bought with a price." So, glorifying God serves as a positive goal for us as we strive for purity.

How does our purity glorify God? It acknowledges:

- The supremacy of God as our creator as we submit to His authority
- The goodness of God who gives His commands for our freedom, not our bondage (John 8:31-32, Romans 6:6-14)
- That God's design for marriage, sex, and our masculinity is for our ultimate good and is more fulfilling than the false intimacy and passing pleasure of impurity
- That God gave us everything necessary to experience life abundantly (John 10:10, 1 Pet.1:3)
- The value of our body as designed by God
- The holiness of our body as the abiding place of the Holy Spirit
- The beauty of the bridegroom-bride relationship of Christ and the church (Eph. 5:31-33)

The fourth positive principle recognizes that our choices should respect us. This may sound weird and selfish, but it is not. Instead, it recognizes the biblical principle that all of me—including my physical body—belongs to God. This choice means I live as the person God designed me to be, the "real me" in Christ, not the person the world and my flesh want me to be. Look again at 1 Cor. 6:19-20: My *body* is the temple of the Holy Spirit, and I am to glorify God *with my body*. Paul adds in 1 Thess. 4:3-4 that we are to abstain from sexual impurity and possess *our own vessel* honorably (probably best understood as our bodies).[35] If we accept the testimony of Scripture, our entire body

---

35 The phrase "possess his own vessel" is difficult to translate. Some take "vessel" to mean "wife" (1 Pet. 3:7). But, the wife is there described as a "weaker" vessel,

(including our sexual organs) has value and our sexual purity honors who we are as God created us.

When we respect ourselves, we also protect our reputation. Think of the many ways sexual sin mars this. How many Christian leaders have destroyed their reputations by falling to some form of sexual sin? In fact, the week before writing this chapter, I heard of yet another pastor who had to give up his ministry after admitting adultery. This man's reputation was gravely wounded. But sexual sin hurts the reputation of any man, not just leaders. Think about how a man hurts his reputation within his own family when his child or spouse discovers him accessing internet pornography or about the impact on his reputation when his marriage crumbles due to sexual sin. Even if a man successfully keeps his struggles with sexual purity private, he is only one slip away from someone discovering his sin and destroying his reputation. Purity prevents this from happening.

The fifth and final positive principle is making choices that honor others, and in particular that honor women. They are not sexual objects for our pleasure. God created women as equal image-bearers with men (Gen 1:27), spiritually equal to men (Gal. 3:28). Wives are described as "co-heirs" with their husbands (1 Pet. 3:7). God designed the first woman to be a "helper" (a positive term, by the way) as the one who "completes" the first man. Women are more valuable than being mere sexual objects for our pleasure. They are real people, with real lives and real feelings. Every woman is someone's daughter and may be a sister, mother, or wife. These descriptions fit *any and every* woman, even those in the sex industry (such as pornography and prostitution). When I choose purity, I honor women as God created them.

---

implying the husband, too, is a vessel. Paul uses the word for the body (2 Cor. 4:7). Thus, it seems most natural to understand Paul's use of the word here as "body," perhaps even a euphemism for male genitals. The verb "possess" carries the meaning "to gain control of." See Gordon D. Fee, *The First and Second Letters to the Thessalonians*, The New International Commentary on the New Testament (Grand Rapids, MI: Wm. B. Eerdmans Publishing Co., 2009), 147, and Charles A. Wanamaker, *The Epistles to the Thessalonians: A Commentary on the Greek Text*, New International Greek Testament Commentary (Grand Rapids, MI: W.B. Eerdmans, 1990), 152–153.

When we are sexually pure, we honor the institution of marriage and the married man honors his wife. Our purity recognizes God designed the "one flesh" intimacy of marriage as the avenue for true sexual fulfillment. When our wives know we look for sexual satisfaction apart from them, they see it as a statement that they are sexually inadequate:

> Women feel threatened by their partner's preoccupation with pornography. These 'other' women, even though they are only pictures, intrude into the marriage relationship. It feels as though your husband is being unfaithful. Even more demeaning is the feeling that you are being compared with these women. And who can compete with airbrushed images that are touched up and unrealistic? The majority of wives can never compete with the lies portrayed in pornography.[36]

Our sexual purity communicates the opposite to our wives. It communicates that we value them. It communicates to her that we believe she alone is our "one-flesh" partner. It communicates to unmarried women that we desire to protect their purity so that should they one day marry, they can enjoy the one-flesh relationship with their future mate. Our actions tell them how highly we value them as a gift from God and as a child of God.

Let's think briefly about the connection between pornography and the principle of honoring women. Sue lamented to me that her husband forced her to watch porn before sex to help "get in the mood." Not only did this use the women in the porn as sex objects (obviously, there was no real relationship with them), but Sue felt demeaned and used as well. She hated the porn and felt unloved by her husband who used other women to "get in the mood." The use of pornography, even if consensual by both man and wife, violates the biblical standard of one man / one woman by inviting the anonymous bodies and faces of those women in the porn into the bedroom.

---

36 Hart, Weber, and Taylor, 185.

> There is one other thing you need to know about these women. I never cared to know their names. It is easy to dehumanize women in adult entertainment. Their reason for existence is to satisfy lust. Nothing more. Their names are insignificant.... Every cent I spent on pornography and adult entertainment was used to keep these women trapped in a world where they were dehumanized, where their value was based on their beauty and their willingness to participate in degrading sexual activities.[37]

Pornography does not and cannot honor women. The women in the photographs or movies are dishonored anytime someone looks at them because the viewer has objectified them, turning them into sexual objects for his fantasies and pleasure. However, we can honor these women by refusing to objectify them, refusing to view the pornography, and thinking of them as God thinks of them and not as the camera sees them.

Think of the concept of honoring others in very practical terms. Once again, you access woo_hoo_hoo_xxx.com. An image appears. How might you respond if you think of the woman in the picture as a sexual toy for your pleasure? Now, rethink how you might respond if you tell yourself, "She is a unique creation created in God's image. And, she is someone's daughter." Imagine one step further—would you want your wife or daughter to do whatever the woman in the image is doing?[38] I suspect the two responses would differ significantly. The first is selfish; the second honors the woman in the picture—even if she is acting dishonorably.

"Wait," I hear someone arguing. "I'm only looking at a woman, not pornography. How does that dishonor women?" A young lady I know sheds light on this with her recent unsolicited post on Facebook:

---

37 Henry J. Rogers, *The Silent War: Ministering to Those Trapped in the Deception of Pornography* (Green Forest, AR: New Leaf Press, Inc., 1999), 68-69.

38 I realize some small percentage of men, those who have had inappropriate incestuous relations with family, might say "yes." If perchance this describes you, continue reading the book, but I strongly recommend you get additional help.

A friendly reminder to co-workers, colleagues, acquaintances, etc.: It is rude to stare, or even "sneak" repetitive, lingering glances, at a woman's breasts. Please don't think that we don't see it. We notice every. single. time. [*sic*] Chances are good that we will not say anything, because it's awkward to talk about and you're definitely going to deny it, making things much, much more awkward. Chances are good that it won't have a huge impact on whether or not we will laugh at your jokes or talk to you during coffee breaks or be as friendly as usual because, honestly, this happens too often to be icy to every person who has this habit. But even if we don't correct you outright and even if we are still friendly, we do not forget those who insist on acting this way again and again. Please, just don't.[39]

The last statement in the description of purity defines the breadth of application of the six previous principles: *I experience purity to the degree that I make godly choices . . . that I act on with my heart, mind, eyes, and actions.* In other words, purity involves my entire being. It involves what I desire, what I think, where I look, what I do, and everything in between. Sound like a very high standard? Absolutely! But remember, God's character defines the standard for our character, "but like the Holy One who called you, be holy yourselves also in all your behavior; because it is written, 'You shall be holy, for I am holy'" (1 Pet. 1:15-16). Not only does the standard seem very high, but it also seems impossible to reach. That's where the seemingly odd phrase "to the degree that" comes into play.

Sexual purity is but one dimension of our spiritual life, and sexual transgressions are but one form of sin. In his first epistle, John makes some seemingly contradictory statements about sin in general that fit our topic: "My little children, I am writing these things to you so that you may not sin. And if anyone sins, we have an Advocate with the Father, Jesus Christ the righteous" (1 Jn. 2:1). John does not want his readers to sin, and he never gives permission to do so, but he also acknowledges that they will sin.

---

39 Used with permission; source information withheld by request.

Some of John's readers might have thought his insistence on the sinfulness of Christians somehow would discourage holiness. The opposite was John's intention . . . But sin is nevertheless a reality, however much John wished his readers would not commit it . . . John did not want his readers to sin, but he knew that none of them was perfect and that all would need the help available from their Advocate.[40]

That's part of the tension of life on this earth as a believer. We might never reach the target of never sinning, but it serves as the right target anyway. As we grow as a believer and more consistently "walk by the Spirit," (addressed in Chapter Six), we will sin less often and take sin more seriously.

In the description of purity, the phrase "to the degree that" recognizes this same tension in our goal to experience purity. On the one hand, I want to experience perfect purity consistently, and I want you to experience the same. On the other hand, I recognize that we occasionally fail. We may have streaks of time that we do well and streaks of time that we do less well. Knowing that we may fail *never* gives us permission *to* fail, just as the writers of Scripture never give the believer permission to sin. However, "to the extent that" recognizes that achieving purity (for most of us) requires growth and time. The phrase "to the extent that" evaluates how we are doing as a lifestyle. However, we must use caution to avoid justifying individual failures by thinking that "overall" we are doing well. Each failure is an act of impurity, a sin. We cannot excuse individual failures by looking at our overall behavior. But at the same time, we cannot let those acts of failure destroy our growth. It is a fine line in our thinking. We can get ourselves in trouble by giving either too little weight or too much weight to our failures. I will address in Chapter Eleven what we should do when we fail.

---

40 Zane C. Hodges, "1 John," in John F. Walvoord, and Roy B. Zuck, ed, *The Bible Knowledge Commentary: An Exposition of the Scriptures* (Wheaton, IL: Victor Books, 1985), 1 John 2:1.

Set your goals high, but do not be surprised if you fail. Purity is experienced "to the extent that . . ." The better we apply the principles in the description, the closer our experiential purity matches the ideals of Scripture; the worse we apply the principles, the further our experience from the ideal.

There are some other benefits to purity. When I make godly choices regarding my sexuality:

- I know I am doing right.

- I know I'm living life the way God designed it.

- I won't have to face guilt or any other negative consequences.

- I won't have memories of past relationships or sexual images haunting me.

- I will have more time and energy for other pursuits.

- I can look my wife (if I am married) or my girlfriend (if I am single) in the eyes without feeling hypocritical.

Keep in mind that experiencing sexual purity does not come free. Jesus called it "counting the cost" (Luke 14:25-33). If we want to make any changes in our life, we do the work towards making those changes because we believe the result is worth the cost required to achieve the change. Several years ago, I wanted to run a 10K race. I had three goals, two serious and the third tongue-in-cheek. First, I wanted to run the entire 10K (6.2 miles) without stopping. Second, I wanted to run it in less than one hour. This was not a record pace by any stretch of the imagination, but for me, it was a challenge to run that quickly! Third, I did not want to die in the process of running; I wanted to live to tell about the race.

The goals were positive. But, I did not just head to the race that Saturday morning and successfully run a 10K in under an hour. I had to train for it. That meant giving up some things I enjoyed (did you know eating Mexican food just before running is not a wise choice?). It meant I had to use some of my free time to train. It meant I had to begin the running process several months before the race to build my stamina. It meant I had to be aware of potholes in the street and dogs loose in the neighborhood. But, the final goal was worth it to me, so

I worked through the process of preparing for the race. And it *was* worth it: I achieved all three of my goals.

What does this have to do with sexual purity? Just as I incurred costs to achieve my goals of successfully running the 10K, I also incur costs to experience sexual purity successfully. We will "give up" certain things to experience purity. One writer describes the price paid for sexual purity this way:

> I want you to consider the cost of moral purity. If you've been hooked on pornography, prostitution, homosexuality, a romantic affair, or a host of other sexual sins, changing your lifestyle won't be easy. Even if you've not gone that far but find yourself thinking more and more about your sexual fantasies, returning to sexual purity won't be easy. Choosing to be pure means giving up something you enjoy. It means saying no to an intense craving for impure sexual pleasure. Simply put, moral purity demands commitment.[41]

Moses gives us an example of "counting the cost":

> By faith, Moses, when he had grown up, refused to be called the son of Pharaoh's daughter, choosing rather to endure ill-treatment with the people of God than to enjoy the *passing pleasures of sin*, considering the reproach of Christ greater riches than the treasures of Egypt; for he was looking for the reward. (Heb. 11:24-25, emphasis added).

Moses knew the reward of obedience was greater than the cost he paid. He refused to be called the son of Pharaoh's daughter. As viewed through Egyptian eyes, Moses gave up a lot: wealth, power, being part of the royal family. And, he gave up the passing *pleasures* of sin. The passage does not tell us the specifics of these sins, but by not sinning, Moses gave up some experience of pleasure. The principle

---

41 Bill Perkins, *When Good Men are Tempted* (Grand Rapids: Zondervan Publishing, 1997), 96.

is clear: sometimes doing the right thing means giving up something pleasurable. As one pastor astutely observed, "If sin weren't fun, people wouldn't do it!" Moses paid a significant cost for the more significant benefit of the reward!

In the area of sexual sin, this principle is crucial to understand. The appropriate expression of sex is very pleasurable, but inappropriate sexual expression can be very pleasurable as well. The physical intensity and pleasure of orgasm do not depend on the appropriateness of the sex. Because the pleasure of sex is powerful, we may sacrifice some real pleasure for the sake of purity.

What might we give up for the sake of purity?

- We will give up the passing pleasure of inappropriate sexual activity.

- We may need to change habits we have practiced for years (such as allowing our eyes to wander over the figure of a woman).

- We may need to find means of dealing with stress and other issues in ways other than sexual release.

- We may face boredom during the time we used to spend pursuing sexual pleasures.

- We may need to give up, limit, or filter access to visual stimuli, such as cable television, movies, and the internet.

- We may face ridicule from others who do not understand what we are doing. We might even lose friends or a girlfriend who do not like the direction we are taking in our life.

- We must persevere in the sheer discipline of walking in purity every day, even those days when we may not feel like it.

- If we've become sexually addicted, we must combat the physical dependencies we've developed.

We also need to be aware that to walk in sexual purity as God designed it, is counter-cultural, swimming upstream so to speak. We live in a culture where pornography is rampant, and accessing it is assumed by most as "acceptable." We live in a culture where sex in dating is considered normal. We live in a culture driven by individualism, a culture that "does not dictate a set of behavioral choices but instead seeks to remove the cultural and social limits on behavior. What it will not abide, however, is any person or group seeking to impose ideas on someone else."[42] We live in a culture that *defines* our sexuality rather than recognizing our divine design:

> Our inherited gender was once seen as normative for determining what form of sex we engaged in and with whom. But it has become a core modern intuition that 'gender' and 'sexuality' are *things we choose*, or that our 'orientation' is part of a deeper 'sexual personality' that transcends our gender.[43]

Hopefully, you now agree sexual purity means more than *not* doing certain things and you see the benefit and power of the positive goals in the description of purity:

I experience purity to the degree that I make godly choices

- *by avoiding all inappropriate sexual activity*
- *by enjoying appropriate expressions of masculinity*
- *by enjoying appropriate relations with the opposite sex*
- *that glorify God*
- *that respect me*
- *that honor others*
- *that I act on with my heart, mind, eyes, and actions*

We all face temptations to turn away from purity to sexual sin. That's the topic of our next chapter—the storms of temptations.

---

42 Dale S. Kuehne, *Sex and the iWorld: Rethinking Relationship beyond [sic] an Age of Individualism* (Grand Rapids, MI: Baker Academic, 2009), 68.

43 Jonathan Grant, *Divine Sex: A Compelling Vision for Christian Relationships in a Hypersexualized Age* (Grand Rapids, MI: Brazos Press, 2015), 121, emphasis added.

CHAPTER THREE

FACING THE STORMS

We can be stormproof men.

Storms are a regular part of the weather. For years, I lived in Louisiana; a state hit hard by two hurricanes in 2005. The first, Katrina, flooded New Orleans and caused untold damage along the Louisiana and Mississippi coasts. A few months after Katrina, Rita struck the coast near Lake Charles. None of the residents affected by these two hurricanes wanted these storms to strike them. They just came. However, with the benefit of modern technology, people knew the storms were coming and could prepare for them. The wise choice for those living directly on the coast or in low-lying areas was to flee the storms rather than risk their wrath. Those who chose this option gathered their valuable belongings, did what they could to protect their homes, and headed inland. Some did not heed the warnings; some lost their lives. Whether facing a hurricane or any other storm, preparation for the storm influences how it impacts us.

Just as storms are a normal part of the weather, so too sexual temptations are a regular part of life. Sexual temptations and natural storms do differ in one significant aspect. When we face the storms of nature, we simply hope to minimize any damage we might incur. We aren't promised relief from the storm, and sometimes, despite our best preventative actions, we still suffer property damage or injury. When a strong thunderstorm rolls over my home, I hope to have adequate time to move my cars into the garage, secure anything that is loose in the backyard, and make sure I plugged all my electrical appliances into surge protectors. But I can do nothing to protect my roof from hail-produced damage.

But we can be "stormproof" when we face sexual temptation. We are not limited to *minimizing* the damage, as we are with a physical storm. Rather, God gives us what we need to face temptation successfully and *prevent* damage. He promises a "way of escape" (1 Cor. 10:13); He promises that by walking by the Spirit, we will not carry out the desire of the flesh (Gal. 5:16). We can withstand the power of temptation.

Before looking at some of the storms men face, let's understand what the Bible means when it speaks of temptation.[44] At its core, temptation entices us to sin or do evil. God is never the source of this enticement:

> Let no one say when he is tempted, 'I am being tempted by God'; for God cannot be tempted by evil, and He Himself does not tempt anyone. But each one is tempted when he is carried away and enticed by his own lust. Then when lust has conceived, it gives birth to sin; and when sin is accomplished, it brings forth death. (James 1:13-16)

Second, temptation falls under two broad categories:

> We must recall that the concept of temptation is both objective and subjective. When someone tries to persuade us to do wrong, he is, *objectively* speaking, tempting us . . . But at the same time, subjectively speaking, we may not be 'tempted,' since all his efforts may not awaken in us any desire to do the particular evil he suggests.[45]

---

44 The Greek verb translated "tempt" (*peirazō*) can also be translated "test." The difference between these two translations (testing or tempting) depends on the intended result of the test/temptation in the context of the verse. A *test* intends to show the true nature or character of the one being tried; *temptation* intends to cause one to stumble. It is an enticement to sin or to do evil.

45 Zane C. Hodges, *The Epistle of James: Proven Character Through Testing* (Irving, TX: Grace Evangelical Society, 1994), 27-28.

These terms—objective and subjective—seem dry and academic, so think of them instead as "external" temptations and "internal" temptations. *Objective* temptations are those external sources which seek to entice us to sin or do evil. They just exist; they pop into our world without invitation. They include those temptations external to our bodies (such as a provocative, unsolicited email) and those random thoughts that seem to pop into our thinking without cause. *Subjective* temptation occurs when we internalize the temptation and begin being carried away by its enticement. For example, sexual temptation crosses from being external to internal when we start dwelling on the thought that popped in our head, maybe fantasizing about it or beginning to plan to act on it. "External" temptations are largely out of our control; "internal" temptations, however, are a different story. Our experience of purity hinges on keeping "external" temptations external and dealing with "internal" temptations healthily.

Bass fishing provides a perfect illustration of the difference between external and internal temptation. I love fishing one particular pond in Texas with my friend Frank. We know that some good-sized bass live in the pond, so when we fish there, I take the tackle I think will attract and catch fish. I usually start by casting a plastic worm along the shore, hoping to grab the eye of an unsuspecting bass. This is "external" (*objective*) temptation—the worm simply shows up in the bass's world, and the bass has no control over its appearance. Thus far, from the fish's perspective, no damage is done. The fish may simply ignore the bait, and my "outside" temptation (the plastic worm) has induced no "internal" response (a strike). I *really* want the bass to be carried away by his lust and then attack the bait. I want him to think, "That looks good . . . I'll eat it!" Once he takes the bait, I set the hook, and the fish is in trouble. He fights, trying to dislodge the hook. The logical end for this fish is death—on the hook, in the net, into the boat, and eventually into the frying pan. What started out as a mere temptation ("That looks good") ended in death. Subjective, "internal" temptation has the same power over us. When we allow our lusts to be enticed, we'll take the bait (be "carried away"), resulting in sin and its consequences.

Objective sources of temptation never come from God. God will not entice his children towards sexual sin. Two of our spiritual enemies—

the world and the devil—regularly throw external sexual temptations in our path. But the real power of temptation lies with the third enemy, the flesh (Rom. 13:14, Gal. 5:13-19). *Internal* temptation is the response of *my* lusts to an external temptation.

I faced one such "external" temptation one night in Atlanta. I was in a motel room the night before speaking about sexual purity at a men's retreat. That evening, two sporting events I wanted to watch were on TV at the same time, on different channels. I didn't know which channels carried either event, so I channel-surfed to find them. After finding the first, I continued to surf, looking for the second. BAM! On one of the stations in between the two, a full frontal nude popped up. That's external temptation—she just appeared while I was doing something innocently. Had I stopped and watched for a while or dwelt on the image in my thinking, this "external" temptation would have become "internal," appealing to my lusts. That first appearance was strictly out of my control (nothing on the channel guide indicated this kind of programming), but any further interaction with it *was*.

The difference between the two types of temptation is important. Because of the world we live in, it is impossible to avoid all external temptation. We can reduce how much comes across our path, but some *will* cross our path. Facing external temptations, however, does not necessarily mean we must succumb to them. Jesus perfectly models that external temptations, even those brought directly from Satan, can be endured without sinning (Matt 4:1-11).

But what happens when we *do* succumb to an external temptation?

The logical end of sin is death. James makes that clear. But a significant majority of men who took my survey indicated they occasionally yielded to some form of sexual temptation and not one of those men died. Does that mean James' warning that sin leads to death is wrong? No! Here are three reasons why: (1) people do not always experience the full possible consequences of their sin, (2) people do not always experience the consequences of their sin immediately, and (3) "death" does not always mean "physical death."

Charles Bing identifies seven different kinds of death:[46]

Kind of death	Separation of:	Examples
1. Physical	Body from spirit	John 19:33; Acts 12:23
2. Spiritual	Unbeliever from God spiritually	Gen. 2;17; Rom. 5:12; Eph. 2:2
3. Experiential	Believer from God in fellowship	Rom. 6:16, 21, 23
4. Second	Unbeliever from God eternally	Rev. 20:14-15
5. Uselessness	Something from its vitality	Heb. 11:12; Jas. 2:20, 26
6. Positional	Believer's new man from sin and the law	Rom. 6:11
7. Powerlessness	Believer from Christ's victorious life and Spirit	Rom. 7:9-11, 24; 8:2, 6, 13

Of these, the believer may experience physical death, experiential death, uselessness, or powerlessness (numbers 1, 3, 5, and 7 under "Kind of death"). And, although the Bible does not use the word "death" for this, a believer may also experience relational death with other persons (e.g., broken fellowship or even a complete separation from the individual, as occurs in a divorce). Even though the believer may not experience physical death, he will experience some degree

---

46 Charles C. Bing, *Grace, Salvation, And Discipleship: How to Understand Some Difficult Passages* (NP: Grace Theology Press, 2015), 49.

of death. Plus, the sinning believer may well suffer other negative consequences as well, such as:

- God's discipline as a loving father who corrects His children (Heb 12:3-6)

- Guilt (true and false)

- Hardening of the heart towards God and the things of God (Heb 3:13)

- Physical issues, such as loss of job, disease, injury, etc.

Let's look at some of the typical storms of temptation we face. As we do so, ask yourself the question (*honestly*), "Is this a temptation with which I struggle?" Keep in mind this section does not list every sexual temptation a person may face. If you struggle with something not addressed, be honest and include your *issue* in the list of these temptations. By identifying typical struggles, we prepare ourselves for when they strike. The rest of the book will help us face the storms and stand strong, to be "stormproof."

Rain showers

You may think this first type of storm doesn't fall under the category of temptation; that they aren't issues that cause you to act out. In and of themselves, rain showers are pretty minor. However, if I have a leak in my roof, even small rain showers cause damage, allowing water where water should not be. In the realm of sexual temptation, rain showers might seem insignificant, but like the home with the leaky roof, they cause damage. They feed us sexual messages, building a baseload of sexual tension in our thinking. If we choose to watch sex scenes in movies, or scantily clad women in magazines (even if they are not nude) or even if we intentionally watch advertisements for that famous lingerie company, then the "roof leaks." We feed our flesh and develop a tolerance for sexual sin. Then, when we face more significant, powerful storms, sex already permeates our mind, and we are less able to battle them.

For example, in many movies and television shows, relationships between men and woman go something like this: Meet someone, become attracted to them, have sex, then (maybe) develop a deeper relationship with them and then sometimes, but only sometimes, get married. Life imitates art, so it is not surprising that our culture often follows the same pattern. Sex becomes something expected in a relationship, not something saved for marriage. In one popular sitcom, the characters wrestled with the question of how often you were supposed to go out with someone before you should expect sex. I doubt anyone would watch the show and then pressure their date to have sex with them because they had gone out more times than the "magic number." However, this show (along with many others) plants the message "sex and dating go together." In another popular show which aired for twelve seasons, the main character is a hedonistic man living a free-wheeling life. He jumps from one casual relationship to another. These messages, repeatedly communicated from many different sources, subtly (or not so subtly!) paint a picture of "normal life," but a "normal" life contrary to God's design.

Be careful of the rain showers. They may not seem like much, but they can saturate the heart and mind with sexual messages, allowing bigger storms to create more havoc.

Ask yourself: Do I allow rain showers in my life? Do I intentionally watch movies with sexual content? Do I "read" the magazines with scantily-clad women? Do I need to be more aware of sexual messages pouring into my life and should I filter them more and tolerate them less?

The eye of the storm, or, the storm of the eyes!

Imagine being a fighter pilot on a combat mission. An enemy aircraft appears in the sky, and your radar tracks him. Soon, you have him locked on, and you are ready to fire. On the ground, our male eyes often act like that radar, but instead of seeking enemy aircraft they, detect female bodies. They lock on, stay locked on, admiring body parts, sometimes hoping for a peek of more. Almost all men face the temptation of the "wandering eye." We expect men to notice women since men are visually stimulated. But this same natural tendency can easily become a problem for us. One man jokingly told me, "Since it's the second glance that becomes a problem, make sure the first glance is a good one!" Noticing an attractive female is not an issue. A lingering look is, however!

You probably don't have to think too hard to know what it means to "lock on" with our eyes. It could be checking out the figure of a woman at the beach or noticing the girl wearing form-fitting jeans or a tight sweater. It could be seeing—and staring at—the cleavage revealed by the top she is wearing. Or it could be checking out any girl that crosses your path, focusing on parts below her neck! The problem is not the women; it is us controlling our eyes, keeping them where they belong.

Ask yourself: Do I find my eyes locking on where and when they shouldn't? Do I feel like my eyes have a mind of their own? Do I justify my wandering eyes with words like, "Wandering eyes are normal for a guy"?

Severe Storm Alert

Sometimes, the weatherman predicts severe weather when a cold front approaches. This front might bring severe thunderstorms, heavy rain, frequent lightning, hail and maybe even tornadoes. When this happens, I watch weather radar and observe the colors on the screen. Green is fine, but orange is more intense, red even more so, and so on. If it looks like something severe will strike near us, I start thinking about how to protect my family. In other words, my thinking focuses on the storm and almost nothing else.

Such a focus is appropriate when it concerns weather conditions and safety. But what if the focus is sex and little else? It has been said that the mind is the biggest sex organ. Men often think of sex (so do women, but typically less often and in different ways, but that's beside the point). You may have heard of the middle-school sex education teacher who told his class, "The average middle school boy thinks about sex at least once every five minutes." One boy smiles, raises his hand, and brags, "Finally! I am an over-achiever!" Something pushes our thoughts toward the sexual. Regardless of our age, sexual thoughts—often inappropriate sexual thoughts—barge into our minds without prompting. Many men agree that *they* think like this! The thought might be a fantasy about someone ("I wonder what she looks like underneath those jeans" or "I wonder if she would . . ."). It might be a memory of pornography viewed earlier. One man came to me following a workshop I gave. "Roger, how do I get rid of the memories I have of the past? I want a pure mind. I don't want my wife to know. I don't want to think about someone else; I don't want to compare my wife with other women. I have all these thoughts floating in my mind, and I can't get rid of them! What can I do?"

Ask yourself: Do I find my thoughts going where I know they shouldn't go? Do I feed my mind with sexual images or stories? Do I find it difficult to stop the sexual thoughts?

Hurricane Warning

Hurricanes inflict damage in countless ways. The tidal surge, wave action, heavy winds, torrential rain, inland flooding, thunderstorms, tornadoes, hail, and the sheer size of the storm wreak havoc wherever it goes. In fact, in the ten-year period ending in 2011, each of thirteen separate hurricanes inflicted over $1 billion damage to the United States.[47] When the National Hurricane Center issues hurricane warnings and evacuation orders, they do so knowing the physical devastation and personal harm the hurricane could inflict. They want the public to take the warnings seriously.

In the realm of sexual temptations, what storm parallels a hurricane?

Pornography!

Pornography inflicts untold havoc wherever it lands. Sadly, more and more of our culture act like those who refuse to take hurricane

---

47 http://www.infoplease.com/ipa/A0882823.html, accessed February 20, 2012.

warnings seriously and instead sit out the storm. Many find porn use acceptable:

> So is porn use an issue among emerging adults? Absolutely. Pornography use is highest among this demographic . . . [R]esearchers interviewed 813 emerging adults—undergraduate and graduate students . . . ranging in age from 18 to 26. Two out of three men agreed that porn use was generally acceptable, while the same was true of half the women.[48]

Not only is it accepted, it permeates the culture:

> Today, pornography is so seamlessly integrated into popular culture that embarrassment or surreptitiousness is no longer part of the equation . . . The all-pornography, all the time mentality is everywhere in today's pornified culture—not just in cyberspace and *Playboy* magazines.[49]

And it seems the percentage who find it acceptable is growing: "While 60 percent of adults age fifty-nine and older believe pornography is demeaning toward women, only 35 percent of Gen-Xers—the most tolerant and often heaviest users—agree."[50]

What constitutes porn? Defining it is not easy. "In 1964, Justice Potter Stewart tried to explain 'hard-core' pornography, or what is obscene, by saying, 'I shall not today attempt further to define the kinds of material I understand to be embraced . . . [b]ut I know it when I see it.'"[51] For our purposes, "porn" includes any media which focuses on explicit sexual content—nudity, sex acts, sexual stories. Any form can carry it—DVD's, magazines, the internet, "sexting," cell phones,

---

48 Regnerus and Uecker, 95.

49 Pamela Paul, *Pornified: How Pornography is Transforming Our Lives, Our Relationships, and Our Families,* (New York: Times Books, 2005), (New York, NY: Times Books, 2005), 4-5.

50 Ibid., 81.

51 http://library.findlaw.com/2003/May/15/132747.html, accessed February 20, 2012

televisions, theaters. The images might be of someone we know (such as "sexting") or a complete stranger. And within the world of porn, no sex act is off limits.

Some might be wondering, "How much nudity is necessary for something to be pornographic?" If our goal is purity, a precise definition is not required. The question is not whether sex and nudity are "tasteful" sex and nudity ("art") or hard-core porn. The questions should start with, "Is there sex or nudity?" If yes, the next question is, "Does what I am viewing nudge me (or flat out push me!) in the direction of sexual impurity?" *Any* storm causes damage, no matter whether the world considers it porn or art. In this case, the problem is how what I observe impacts what I think.

The porn industry is a multi-billion dollar enterprise. Obtaining reliable numbers is notoriously difficult, but

> [A] detailed meta-analysis done by Covenant Eyes . . . shows that in 2005 and 2006, the United States pornography industry generated $12.62 and $13.33 billion in revenue respectively. This encompassed video sales and rentals, internet, cable, pay-per-view, in-room, mobile, phone sex, exotic dance clubs, novelties, and magazines.
>
> So what about now, in 2012? Very little research has been done recently into the size of the pornography industry. For instance, a 2012 Time article quoted an estimate by the Adult Video Network . . . at $2.8 billion. Note that this does not indicate what exactly was included in the study, only noting that it was the "online" adult entertainment industry.
>
> Keeping these studies in mind and the massive amount of free internet pornography available, let's conservatively estimate the U.S. pornography industry at around $8 billion.[52]

---

52 http://www.covenanteyes.com/2012/06/01/how-big-is-the-pornography-industry-in-the-united-states/, accessed August 10, 2107.

This analysis does show that revenues have dropped in the last decade, largely due to the availability of free on-line pornography.[53] The sheer volume of porn, its accessibility (much at no cost and available through any device that can connect to the internet), its anonymity (there is no interpersonal contact when accessing porn online), and its acceptance by much of our culture make pornography an incredibly powerful temptation against our purity.

To see the damage inflicted by porn, look at the difference between what porn teaches and the description of purity given earlier:

> *I experience purity to the degree that I make godly choices by avoiding all inappropriate sexual activity.* Porn redefines sex, turning it into no more than a physical act between any number and combination of people. It ignores that sexuality is part of who the person is, that it is not "just something they do." It ignores romance and tenderness. It ignores God's design for sex between one man and one woman within the boundaries of marriage.

> *I experience purity... by enjoying appropriate expressions of masculinity.* Porn portrays any variety of sex as the ultimate masculine experience. And those who watch porn usually masturbate:

>> For most men, pornography is... an easy way to get off. Men generally masturbate while they are looking at pornography, or immediately after, unless they are at work... Not a single man who looked at pornography interviewed for this book did so without masturbating at least some of the time.[54]

---

53 Global expenditures in 2006 approached $100 billion, of which the United States contributed about 14%. Assuming global expenditures dropped at the same rate as U.S. expenditures between 2006 and 2012, global expenditures would still exceed $50 billion. (http://www.familysafemedia.com/pornography -statistics/#anchor1, accessed August 10, 2017).

54 Paul, 25-26.

Neither sex as portrayed in porn nor the response of men who watch the porn fits as an "appropriate expression of masculinity."

I experience purity . . . by enjoying appropriate relations with the opposite sex. Porn is selfish and anonymous, not relational. It turns women into sexual objects and does not enhance relationships. In fact, it hurts real relationships.

I experience purity . . . by glorifying God. Porn violates God's design for sex as an expression of love and intimacy. Porn effectively denies that God's design for sex comes *from* a good God *for* our good. It portrays biblical sex as narrow-minded and outdated. Watching any sex voyeuristically does not honor God.

I experience purity . . . by respecting me. Porn dishonors the one watching by creating sexual memories within him, apart from experiences with his wife. It creates false expectations for sex and feeds self-centered thinking. It can even alter his brain chemistry, sometimes resulting in porn addiction.[55]

I experience purity . . . by honoring women. Porn dishonors women by objectifying them and using them. It creates a false definition of intimacy, that intimacy is merely the physical act between people.

Ask yourself: Do I search the internet for porn? If so, how often (be honest)? Do I hide my electronic device use from others? Do I spend money and time accessing porn? Do I purchase magazines or DVDs? Do I visit "adult" stores or theaters? How much time do I spend viewing porn?

---

55 Gary Wilson, *Your Brain on Porn: Internet Pornography and the Emerging Science of Addiction* (NP: Commonwealth Publishing, 2014), Chapter Two, Kindle.

More bad weather

Some use chat rooms, instant messaging, texting and other conversational technology to engage in sexual activity of all kinds. Not surprisingly, when a person is communicating with a stranger, they may discover that the person is not who she portrays herself to be. A few years ago, my hometown paper reported the bust of an internet pornography ring within the city. Sitting at the computer was an overweight, middle-aged man in his underwear portraying himself to the person calling as an 18-year-old girl!

Some temptations may involve more overt activity and may include the participation of others. Some men become sexually active in their dating relationships. Some choose to live with their girlfriends. Culturally, this lifestyle is becoming more and more acceptable. But, if God's design for sex is within marriage, cohabitation bypasses this crucial step. Some men pursue voyeurism ("peeping Toms"). Some men pick up prostitutes. Some hook up for casual sex. Some pursue adulterous affairs. Some become exhibitionists ("flashers"). Some pursue bi-sexual or same-sex relations. And some face other temptations not mentioned in this book. But whether or not we've addressed the particular temptations you face, it is important to identify them to withstand them better when the temptation does come.

> *Ask yourself:* Which temptations cause me to struggle? Which ones do I pursue?

There is one more hurricane-force storm faced by some men. They face the same temptations as other men, but face the added issue of addiction. This book is useful for the sex addict, but overcoming sexual addiction requires more than we will cover. Chapter Eleven says more about addiction.

Let's think about *when* we expect certain weather patterns to strike. I now live in Texas. I never worry about ice storms in July, but I do look for ice or snow in January or February. The risk of tornadoes in December is low, but the risk increases significantly in the spring when warm, moist air collides with colder air, producing severe thunderstorms. If I know the weatherman predicts cold, wind, and rain tomorrow, I will not wear shorts or drive in my car with the top down! *Knowing* when the storms are coming helps us to be alert and to be better prepared for them. Many sexual temptations are like these weather systems in that they, too, are "seasonal." If I scrutinize my life, I can identify times and circumstances when temptations are most likely to strike. Let's look at three hypothetical examples:

Example #1: I am on a business trip out of town. Almost every motel room includes cable television with access to one or more movie networks. Many include pay-per-view movies, including pornographic films. Usually, when I am at a conference or on a business trip, I stay in the room by myself. Even if I meet someone for dinner, at the end of the day, I am alone in the room. Sometimes, I feel lonely. I resist surfing the previews for the movies, but eventually curiosity wins, and I surf them (okay, my flesh won, not my curiosity). I discover that the motel does not list the movie title on my room bill. I begin to fantasize about watching an adult movie, and I finally order it. In this case, I am most susceptible to this temptation when I am alone, when I feel tired, and when I feel little risk of getting caught.

Example #2: I am married, but my marriage relationship is less than ideal. Our sex life frustrates me. We don't make love as often as I like, and many times the sex does not seem satisfying. My wife fell asleep, and I am alone, awake, and wanting sex. So I slip out of the bedroom, go to my office, close the door, and access "woo_hoo_hoo_xxx.com." I spend an hour indulging in porn, and I end the night by masturbating. I know it's not right, but I also know sex with my wife is out of the question for tonight. I rationalize to myself that I haven't hurt anyone. In this case, I am most susceptible when my wife and I are struggling in our relationship.

Example #3: Work was tough this week. I didn't get the promotion I wanted. The long hours are getting to me. To top it off, I feel stress because I've maxed out my credit card and I'm trying to figure out how to pay all the bills with the money we have. I feel discouraged, tired, and stressed. I'm home alone, so I opt to head to a local strip club. In this case, I am most susceptible when I felt disappointment and inadequate because life did not seem to be going my way.

Ask yourself: Under what circumstances (time, places, and situations) am I most vulnerable? What emotions am I feeling? When is the storm at its worst?

The truth is that most sexual temptations do not blindside us, but because we've never honestly thought about them, we live as if we're helpless and hopeless in the battle. Recognizing patterns in our life is a key. We can then be more proactive in dealing with the circumstances when we face them or in avoiding them in the first place.

We meet "external" (objective) sexual temptation almost regularly in our world. Some of those "external" temptations appeal to our flesh, and the problem then becomes an "internal" (subjective) temptation. That puts us in the midst of the storm. We may (incorrectly) conclude the situation is hopeless, and, as "mere men" we can't possibly help but yield to temptation. As "mere men" that is true, with rare exception. But, we don't battle for purity as "mere men." Recall the promises of 1 Cor. 10:13: "God is faithful and with the temptation will provide a way of escape." We *can* experience purity. God has provided what we need to live as He commands. That's what the rest of the book addresses.

CHAPTER FOUR

THE "M" WORD

Here's something that will surprise no one. Men masturbate. Seventy percent of the men who took my survey—Christian men in solid churches—report they masturbate on some frequency, averaging about six times per month. The frequency of masturbation varies from man to man, but the practice itself is independent of one's station in life. At least two out of three men in every group in my survey said they masturbate on some frequency, whether single or not; active or inactive in practicing their faith; younger (35 years old and younger) or older. In fact, only in the group of men over 65 years old did less than half report they masturbate!

Why do men masturbate? For all kinds of reasons. In my study, about half of the men said they had a strong sex drive; about a quarter said it was a habit; almost 40 percent said they had no other sexual outlet, and almost 40 percent said they merely enjoyed it or felt aroused. And yet, despite the high number of men who admit to masturbating, most of them feel ill at ease with this practice. Almost two-thirds of those who say they masturbate also report they feel guilty, shameful, or abnormal because of masturbating.[56] Do you see the tension here?

---

56 Fankhauser, 106-107.

Remember the words in 1 Corinthians 10:13 that "no temptation has overtaken you but such as is *common to man*"? If we masturbate on any frequency, we are not abnormal; we are not the only man who does so. Just the opposite! A majority do. On the one hand, it helps to know we are not alone but on the other hand, "common" does not define "right." So, as Christians, what do we do with this issue? Is it right? What does the Bible say about the issue?

Scriptures contain no passages that directly condemn or condone masturbation.[57] Whatever conclusion we draw about masturbation must come from applying biblical principles rather than any direct comment from Scripture. In fact, within conservative Christian circles, we find four main positions on the morality of masturbation:

1. It is a gift from God.

2. It is probably alright if not indulged in with lustful fantasies, is not compulsive, is not performed in groups, and does not produce guilt.

3. It is probably (or usually) wrong because it goes against nature and may be a violation of the biblical law of purity.

4. It is always wrong.[58]

What issues should we consider when evaluating the morality of masturbation?[59]

---

57 Sometimes Genesis 38:8-10, the sin of Onan, is used as a proof text against masturbation. The issue in the passage, however, is Onan's failure to provide his brother an heir through levirate marriage, not masturbation.

58 Robert McQuilkin, *Introduction to Biblical Ethics*, 2nd ed., (Tyndale House, 1995), 229. The words "or usually" are mine.

59 These six issues come from a combination of my thoughts and several resources, including Randy C. Alcorn, *Christians in the Wake of the Sexual Revolution: Recovering Our Sexual Sanity* (Portland: Multnomah Press, 1985), Stanley J. Grenz, *Sexual Ethics*, R.K. Harrison, gen. ed., *Encyclopedia of Biblical & Christian Ethics*, rev. ed. (Nashville: Thomas Nelson Publishers, 1992), Hart, *The Sexual Man*, Steve Tracy, unpublished class notes, "Biblical Sexuality," Phoenix Seminary, 1998, and Daniel R. Heimbach, *True Sexual*

- *Fantasy and lust vs. a pure thought life.* Rarely can a man masturbate without some lustful thought or fantasy running through his mind. But Jesus said if a man looks at a woman with lust, he is guilty of sexual sin (Matt. 5:28). Often, some pornography or other inappropriate visual source fuels the lust and fantasy. Masturbation linked with inappropriate thoughts or "lustful passion" (1 Thess. 4:4) is wrong.

- *Intimacy vs. sexual release.* Masturbation is void of any physical and emotional intimacy with another person, contrary to God's design for sex within the one-flesh husband-wife relationship. Sexual pleasure within the context of this marriage relationship is good and is enjoyable. God's design for sex includes both emotional and spiritual intimacy; masturbation results in orgasm (physical release) but no more than that. It does not and cannot build real intimacy with another person. Masturbating to avoid intimacy in a marriage or as a substitute for real intimacy is inappropriate.

- *Satisfying a habit or an addiction vs. self-control.* Masturbation may lead to an unhealthy habitual pattern of sexual release. Our culture rarely teaches self-control, but it is biblical. The fruit of the Spirit includes self-control (Gal. 5:23), and self-control is a mark of a spiritual man (Titus 1:8). Lack of self-control, on the other hand, is one characteristic of ungodly men in the last days (2 Timothy 3:3). Masturbation to satisfy a habit or an addiction is a failure to exercise self-control and is inappropriate.[60]

- *Self-centered sex vs. other-centered sex.* God designed sex for one man with one woman as an expression of intimacy between two people. As Paul points out in 1 Corinthians 7:3-4, sex should express selflessness, not selfishness: The husband's body is his wife's and her body is his. Even the penis

---

Morality: Recovering Biblical Standards for a Culture in Crisis (Wheaton, IL: Crossway Books, 2004).

60 Wilson, *Your Brain on Porn*, passim.

and vagina are naturally designed for one another, as Paul's words "the natural function" imply (Romans 1:26). In fact, we could define sex as "mutual ministry in the bedroom." Masturbation, by definition, requires self-stimulation and therefore ignores both God's other-centered design for sex and the "natural" use of the sexual organs. It is self-centered sex.

- *Deceptive reasoning vs. healthy reasoning.* When testosterone levels climb, men can become pretty creative in justifying masturbation. We may rationalize with lines like "I'm single—I don't have a wife with whom to enjoy sex," or "My wife is tired, and this way I can experience relief and I won't bother her." Or we may convince ourselves that we are entitled to release: "My wife isn't interested in sex as often as I am. I can't help it if I desire sex! I deserve the pleasure and the release." We need to carefully evaluate our thinking and not allow deceptive thinking to control our actions. Healthy reasoning requires an honest evaluation of our motives. Wouldn't it be nice if we had a "baloney detector" that went off when faulty thinking popped in our head? I suspect the vast majority of times (if not *every* time) that we "justified" masturbation this detector would sound off!

- *Damaging sexual relationships vs. enjoying sex in marriage to the fullest.* Regular masturbation, whether by a married man or a single man, may cause problems in the sexual relationship with his wife (or future wife if single). The Song of Solomon pictures a robust relationship between husband and wife, which God designed for couples to enjoy. When someone masturbates, he learns to respond to his own touch instead of that of his wife, which may result in less than satisfying sex when he is with her. Frequent masturbating may bring many problems into the relationship including reduced desire for sex, premature ejaculation, and unrealistic expectations of his partner.

When I consider these principles, I conclude that, based on biblical principles, masturbation is *usually* wrong (the third of the four positions mentioned earlier). I would word it even more strongly—it is *almost always* wrong. I believe exceptions are rare. I believe our aim should be complete abstinence from masturbation, especially since rarely (if ever?) do we do so without inappropriate stimuli or thoughts. However, if masturbation is *usually* wrong, are there any circumstances when might it not be? I *very hesitantly* offer one scenario: the occasional release of sexual pressure if and only if it there are no inappropriate stimuli or thoughts (e.g., lust, pornography, fantasy). I suspect very few can honestly meet these criteria! One author observed, "I know of one man who says he occasionally masturbates purely for the release of a physical pressure but with no sexual thoughts at all, moral or immoral. My conversations with many others indicate this man is the exception, not the rule."[61] I am hesitant to offer even this scenario because I am aware of *no-one* who can keep their thoughts pure while masturbating! Most likely, neither you nor I meet these criteria! So, for the sake of argument, I'll assume for the rest of this chapter that masturbation is wrong. If you think you are the exception, remember this passage: "The heart is more deceitful than all else and is desperately sick; Who can understand it?" (Jer. 17:9). Is your self-assessment true or deceived? You may be the rare exception; just be careful in your thinking.

You might wonder why I don't believe the first two options (that masturbation is a gift from God or that it is probably okay) are good options. Both of these views are difficult to reconcile with the principle of purity. Since men rarely masturbate without some lustful thoughts or fantasy and since masturbation is essentially a selfish act, it seems unlikely that God gave masturbation as a gift or that it is probably alright when the same God said things like:

- "Everyone who looks at a woman with lust for her has already committed adultery with her in his heart" (Matt. 5:28)

---

61 Alcorn, 215.

- "But immorality or any impurity or greed must not even be named among you . . ." or, as the NIV says it, "there must not be *even a hint* of sexual immorality . . ." (Eph. 5:3)

- "Do not merely look out for your own personal interests, but also for the interests of others." (Phil. 4:2).

I've heard some creative attempts to get around these issues. I met with a college-aged single man who said, "I don't lust over anybody when I masturbate. I just imagine a faceless woman. It certainly isn't anyone in particular! So I'm not violating any biblical principles, am I?" He was not happy with me, but agreed with me, when I told him, "It seems to me during this process that you've reduced your view of women to a collection of body parts. Do you think this honors women or honors the biblical principles of purity?"

Another creative attempt argues that masturbation is okay if you are only fantasizing about your future wife. You rationalize that since you are thinking only of the woman who will one day be your wife, you are not *really* violating any biblical principles. As creative as this view may be, it has at least three major problems. First, unless you are already engaged, the fantasy woman is either a faceless collection of body parts or is someone who is not yet your fiancé. Such fantasies fail to honor your future wife. Second, if you are engaged, then you are involved in a form of pre-marital sex, albeit no actual intercourse has occurred. In your mind, you are sexually involved with your fiancé, even though she is not yet your wife. It seems difficult to justify this fantasy sex with Jesus' words in Matthew 5:28 about lust. Third, fantasy sex and real sex differ drastically. The fantasy person does whatever we want, and the "inconveniences" of real sex never pop up. These "inconveniences" are a real part of real sex with a real person. They include things like feeling awkward together, or not enjoying certain actions or positions, or our partner not responding as we might wish, or our partner not being interested in sex whenever we might be. Fantasy sex can create unrealistic expectations about what we should expect in marital sex. Thus, rather than enhancing our future sex life, it may create problems when the real and the fantasy clash in the marriage bed.

If we agree that masturbation is usually wrong, what can we do to improve the probability of abstinence? What are the "ways of escape" which God promises? The seven principles that follow provide a sneak peek of the concepts we'll discuss in the rest of the book. I'm giving the principles here because I want you to see and believe that we can successfully avoid masturbating. We are not helpless or hopeless facing this storm!

1. *Don't fuel the fire.* When we go camping, we usually build a campfire. If we add wood to the fire, it burns higher and longer, but it will die of its own accord if we do not add more wood to it. Our sexual desires are much the same. We "stoke the fires" and then wonder why our desire is so high! The sexual build up we seek to release is often self-induced. We don't avoid known sources of sexual content, or we intentionally pursue sources of sexual content. Even if we don't respond to this content by acting out some way, we have added fuel to the fire. Skills such as choosing to avoid sources of sexual content when possible or diverting the eyes rather than allowing them to linger will reduce much of the pressure.

2. *Learn to endure physical discomfort.* Unreleased physical pressure—particularly after arousal—often serves as a reason for masturbating. Masturbation will relieve the physical pressure, but so will time. Our body and our mind demand sexual release. But, we have a choice. We are not forced to give in; we can say "no." It might not be easy, and it might not be comfortable for some period, but we can overcome the desire. An added benefit of enduring the physical pressure *this* time is that we have greater confidence that we can endure it *next* time!

3. *Practice self-control.* When the urge to masturbate arises, (a) if something is tempting you, flee; (b) change your physical location to reduce the possibility of yielding; and (c) pray. Pray something like: "Holy Spirit, in my flesh, I feel like I can't practice self-control. My flesh *wants* the sexual release. I can experience self-control if you give me the ability to do so. So I am going to depend on You to give me the control

I don't have on my own."[62] When you pray this, don't wait for a *feeling* of God's power. Believe that He has given it to you already, then in faith respond to Him (Chapter Six). Don't give in! Frankly, we may need to pray often like this as we learn to practice self-control.

4. *Allow God's design to take its course.* Keep in mind that sex is not a "need," but instead a strong, natural, desire. I'm aware of no one who has died from lack of sex! Referring to it as a "need" elevates its importance too high in our thinking—even if unintentionally. Many writers point out that the average man "needs" sex about every three days, but I've found no evidence that confirms this "three-day rule." Some men desire sex more often, some less. However, we cannot use this cycle as an excuse for masturbation, "I need sex every three days, and since it's not available, I need to masturbate to relieve the urge." Our desires will fade if we do not give in to sexual temptation.

Many believe nocturnal emissions ("wet dreams") relieve the buildup of seminal fluid and hormones:

> We now know that wet dreams occur without being brought on by masturbation. They are the body's way of taking care of the buildup of seminal fluid that occurs, particularly in young men, and may or may not be connected with erotic dreams. They are an automatic response that cannot be controlled by the individual.[63]

---

62 Adapted from Tony Evans, *The Promise* (Chicago, IL: Moody Press, 1996), 184-185.

63 Clifford & Joyce Penner, 218. See also, Stephen Arterburn and Fred Stoeker, *Everyman's Battle* (Colorado Springs: WaterBrook Press, 2000), 118-119, "Wet Dream FAQ," teens.webmd.com/boys/wet-dream-faq, accessed August 2, 2017, McQuilkin, 228-231. Several sources report the frequency of nocturnal emissions decreases for those who ejaculate during sex or masturbation, reinforcing the idea that these dreams relieve the normal buildup of seminal fluid (e.g., "Wet Dream FAQ").

Most men, and men of all ages, experience these emissions from time to time. The "dreams" are sexual, and our body responds by ejaculating during our sleep. Since most dreams are beyond our control, these nocturnal emissions in themselves are not sinful.[64] Of course, these involuntary ejaculations are messy and usually embarrassing. We can overcome any embarrassment by reminding ourselves that nocturnal emissions are natural and normal, but if we struggle with overcoming these emotions, talk to a counselor or pastor.[65]

5. *Find other avenues of stress reduction*, such as exercising, reading, going out for a cup of coffee (invite a friend!), listening to music, fishing, mowing the yard, or whatever works for you as a stress reliever. Be creative!

6. *Share your struggles with someone you can trust.* James tells us to confess our sins to one another and to pray for one another so we might be healed (James 5:16). Telling a trustworthy friend about your temptations reduces their power and increases your chance of enduring it successfully.

7. *If you are married, work on intimacy with your wife.* If you develop intimacy and a regular sex life with her, the desire to

---

64 We can influence to some degree what we dream by our daytime activities. If we feed our thinking with sexual content, we increase the odds of a sexual dream. However, even though the dream itself is not sinful, as it is not something we control, our actions during the day may well be.

65 I initially included "physician" in this list of people to consult. However, I discussed this section with an internal medicine doctor to confirm its accuracy. I removed it after this comment from him: "If you leave the part about talking with a physician in there you'll probably also want to add a caveat that physicians, in general, were not taught about the physical and psychological harms of pornography and definitely were not formally taught of its spiritual harms, and it is not unheard of for a physician to recommend pornography as a way of dealing with some sexual dysfunctions." (Joel B. Fankhauser, M.D., email message to author, August 12, 2017).

masturbate should lessen. Marriage cannot guarantee that the desire will disappear, especially if we masturbated regularly before the wedding. However, if both husband and wife work on developing real intimacy and experience to some degree what Tim Gardner calls "sacred sex" (sex at its best as designed by God),[66] then the experience of physical intimacy will be more rewarding, and the act of masturbating will be less appealing. Keep in mind, however, that if our marital sex life is less than satisfying for whatever reason, we cannot use that as an excuse to yield to any sexual temptation.

What happens if we still choose to masturbate? We'll usually realize that it provides short-term physical gratification, but not long-term satisfaction. As one author noted, "solo sex is not a healthy substitute for real sex."[67] If we masturbated, we likely had one of two thoughts:

1. We believed we could do it without inappropriate stimuli or thoughts. But use your imaginary "baloney detector" to honestly evaluate your heart (Jer. 17:9). Our capacity to justify any action, including masturbation, is limited only by our imagination!

2. We knew it was wrong but chose to do so anyway. In this case, we should confess our sin (1 John 1:9). "Confess" means to agree with God, or, to say the same thing as God. It is admitting our true guilt before God that we sinned. We are free to enjoy walking in purity again. We'll talk more in Chapter Eleven about dealing with failure.

We need to consider some balancing thoughts before we finish this chapter. Most of us probably remember the adage, "If you don't stop, you'll go blind!" We need to keep this issue in biblical balance. On the one hand, we must not *understate* the seriousness of masturbation. We must deal with it seriously as sin. But on the other hand, we must not

---

66 Gardner, 8.

67 Hart, *The Sexual Man*, 141.

overstate the sinfulness of masturbation. It is *a* sin, not *the* sin. We give certain sins more credit than they deserve and we create more guilt and shame around those sins than we should. We make it difficult for men and especially for adolescents to be open and honest with their struggles. The teenage boy needs to know his struggles are common for his age. He needs help learning how to apply the principles discussed above; he does not need more shame.

All of us—adult and teen alike—need to learn how to deal with masturbation like other sin issues in life. We need to learn how to use the resources God gave us to control it. We need to learn how to deal with our failure if we slip. Masturbation is a temptation "common to man (and teenagers)."

> *Ask yourself:* What is my conclusion about the appropriateness of masturbation? Do I ever masturbate? If so, how often? And, if so, what do I use as my focus when masturbate? Porn? Fantasy? How have I rationalized my actions?

So far, this book has primarily focused on the problems we face regarding impurity, its source in the fallen nature of man, and the temptations faced by men. We now turn to how we can successfully face sexual temptations. However, the solution doesn't start with something we *do*, as the next chapter explores.

CHAPTER FIVE

SOLID AS A ROCK

W e thought every year we lived near the Texas coast was "the" year a hurricane would make landfall near us. That turned out not to be the case, but not too long after we moved from Texas, the eye of a hurricane passed directly over our former home. The question of living along the Gulf Coast was not *whether* a hurricane would strike close enough to affect you, but *when* one would strike close enough to affect you. I am still amazed how many homeowners build near the beach in harm's way, knowing the inevitability of these storms. However, not every storm destroys everything in its path. What factors allow one home to survive when another does not?

One factor is location, location, location! Every year, we see news footage of homes destroyed by a storm somewhere because rushing water, a mudslide, or storm waves eroded the ground beneath the home. Homes built upon solid ground have a greater chance of surviving than those built on less stable ground. Also, building the foundation on the solid ground makes a huge difference. If the foundation is faulty, the main structure has little chance of survival. Finally, using good building materials and building to code increase the odds of the home surviving. Structures built poorly cannot face the onslaught of natural disasters.

What is the connection between a home surviving a storm and our sexual purity? Just this: The right foundation makes all the difference. Storms—sexual temptations—are inevitable. These storms can destroy our sexual purity. If we want to stand pure in the face of these storms, we must begin with a strong foundation. Here is the simple math:

> Our strong male sex drive
>
> + the power of our flesh
>
> + the intensity of the storms of sexual temptation
>
> + the wrong foundation
> _____
>
> = little or no chance for long-term purity.

However, if we build *in* the right place *on* a solid foundation, the math changes:

> Our strong male sex drive
>
> + the power of our flesh
>
> + the intensity of the storms of sexual temptation
>
> + the right foundation
> _____
>
> = great chance for long-term purity.

That "right foundation" is the *unchanging person, power, and provisions of God.*

Put simply, theology matters! An incorrect view of God—the wrong foundation—leads to all kinds of faulty thinking and dangerous practices. We develop an inadequate view of our sinfulness and the consequences of our sin. We fall short in our understanding of the promises and provisions that God gave us to live by, including those that lead to purity. We fail to see a connection between God and the real issues of day-to-day life (such as purity). We rationalize what we are doing ("It's just a natural response"); we minimize what we are doing ("I'm not hurting anyone by looking at porn"). Even worse, we believe we cannot succeed in our purity and give up.

On the other hand, an accurate view of God—the right foundation—leads to sound thinking and practices. Look at the experience of Isaiah:

> In the year of King Uzziah's death I saw the Lord sitting on a throne, lofty and exalted, with the train of His robe filling the temple. Seraphim stood above Him, each having six wings: with two he covered his face, and with two he covered his feet, and with two he flew. And one called out to another and said, 'Holy, Holy, Holy, is the Lord of hosts, The whole earth is full of His glory.' And the foundations of the thresholds trembled at the voice of him who called out, while the temple was filling with smoke. (Isa. 6:1-4)

Re-read this passage slowly. Try to imagine the grandeur of this scene. Imagine the sensory overload Isaiah experienced when he saw the Lord in all His glory, the smoke, the angels, their unending proclamation of the holiness of God, the trembling of the foundation. He had an interesting response to this unbelievable experience:

> Then I said, 'Woe is me, for I am ruined! Because I am a man of unclean lips, And I live among a people of unclean lips; For my eyes have seen the King, the Lord of hosts.' (Isa. 6:5)

He saw God in His glory, understood God's greatness, and saw something about both his own and Israel's sinfulness. But why does Isaiah refer to his unclean lips? The Bible repeatedly says that what comes out of one's mouth indicates what is *in his heart*. In other words, when Isaiah said he was "a man of unclean lips," he acknowledged his sinfulness! Did you notice that not once did God or one of his angels *tell* Isaiah he was sinful? Isaiah recognized it because he saw the glory of God. He understood that he fell short of the glory of God (Rom. 3:23). Because he had an adequate and correct view of God, he had an adequate and correct view of his sinfulness.

God then showed Isaiah something else about His character:

> Then one of the seraphim flew to me with a burning coal in his hand, which he had taken from the altar with tongs. He touched

my mouth with it and said, 'Behold, this has touched your lips; and your iniquity is taken away and your sin is forgiven.' (Isa. 6:6-7)

This is grace! Isaiah did nothing to experience God's grace. God initiated it; Isaiah simply received it, and God forgave Isaiah's sin. Moreover, only *after* Isaiah sees God's holiness and experiences God's grace does God call Isaiah to service: "Then I heard the voice of the Lord, saying, 'Whom shall I send, and who will go for Us?' Then I said, 'Here am I. Send me!'" Isaiah responded correctly to God's call because he had an adequate and correct view of God. Like Isaiah, each of us needs an adequate and correct view of God to make consistently right choices, whether for our purity or any other life decision. That is why we must build our purity on the solid rock of the unchanging person, power, and provisions of God. We need to start with the "who" of God before the "what and how" of our actions.

Let's first consider God's person. Who He truly is.

"I couldn't think about God. I was too ashamed of my sin. So, I had to clean up my life before I could look at Him." Dale had been wrestling with sexual purity for some time. Although he made significant strides forward with this approach, I think he showed some typical misunderstandings of God. It is perfectly normal to feel shame and feel reluctance about coming to God when we are in sin—especially when we knowingly and repeatedly commit the same sin. But just because the response is normal does not make it right! Nowhere in Scripture does God say, "Clean up your act, then come to me." Instead, Jesus offers rest before "cleaning up our act:"

Come to Me, all who are weary and heavy-laden, and I will give you rest. Take My yoke upon you and learn from Me, for I am gentle and humble in heart, and you will find rest for your souls. For My yoke is easy and My burden is light. (Matthew 11:28-30)

You and I will not experience the throne room in the same way as Isaiah. So where do *we* see God? In His Word!

In what follows, I hope to whet your appetite to learn more about our God, especially from the Bible itself. I cannot do justice in one chapter to what the Bible tells us about Him. The best we can do is take a quick tour of some of His attributes.

No list of attributes fully describes God. They help us understand what He is truly like, but He is so much more than the sum of His attributes. Remember, too, that every attribute of God works in perfect harmony with every other attribute of God. We often hear "God is love" (which is true), but God is not *only* love. We know God is holy, yet God is not *only* holy. His love cannot trump His holiness, nor can His holiness trump His love. Every attribute of God works in perfect harmony with every other attribute of God.

- *God is faithful* (Psalm 33:4, 100:5, 1 Cor. 10:13). I recently read through all the Old Testament prophets. Repeatedly, these prophets confront Israel about her sin, and they then foretell the discipline she will receive as a nation because of that persistent sinfulness. Yet, every prophet also reminded Israel that God would not desert the nation, that He would honor the promises He gave Abraham centuries before. God is always completely reliable and trustworthy.

  When He makes a promise, He is *always* faithful to honor that promise. Paul gave us the promise in 1 Cor. 10:13 that "God is faithful, who will not allow you to be tempted beyond what you are able, but with the temptation will provide the way of escape also." We can trust God every time we face a temptation that He will provide that way of escape. Just as He was faithful to Israel, He will be faithful to us.

- *God is holy* (Isa. 6:3, 1 Pet. 1:15-16, Rev. 4:8). "When we say 'God is holy,' we mean He is totally separated from all that is unholy, defiling, or contrary to His nature. God's holiness is unique and distinctive in that it is without any contamination or impurity."[68] But holiness means more than being separated from unrighteousness. It also means God is

---

68 J. Carl Laney, *God* (Nashville, TN: Word Publishing. 1999), 88.

completely pure and righteous; In Him "there is no darkness at all" (1 John 1:5).

God calls us, His people, to be holy because He is holy (1 Pet. 1:15-16). Sexual sin clashes with God's holiness. Sexual purity, on the other hand, reflects the holiness of God and therefore honors Him!

- *God is love* (1 John 4:8). Some words are difficult to define, and "love" is one of those. Most definitions of love sound dry and inadequate. So, rather than try to define it, let's simply look at the most magnificent illustration of God's love: "For God so loved the world, that He gave His only begotten Son, that whoever believes in Him shall not perish, but have eternal life" (John 3:16). This "world" which God loved consists of every person that ever has or ever will live! He gave His Son, who died on the cross for us. As an act of His love, He freely gives eternal life to every person who believes in Him. This particular act of love is completely unmerited—we call it grace (Eph. 2:8-9). Keep in mind that God loved the world despite the sinful condition of all humanity, not because people somehow deserved it. Jesus died for us while we were helpless, ungodly, sinners, and enemies of God (Rom. 5:6-10). The perfectly holy God loved the unholy us. He loved us deeply enough to bring us into His family: "See how great a love the Father has bestowed on us, that we would be called children of God; and such we are" (1 John 3:1). We might not be able to define love, but we see God's love in sending Jesus to die for us. And he died for those treated as mere sex objects, even those in the sex industry.

- *God is good* (Psalm 34:8, 100:5, 118:1, Luke 18:19). God's character is inherently good, and everything God does is good (Psalm 119:68). He never says every circumstance is good, but He does say He will work everything *for* good (Rom. 8:28). Sometimes we see how God does this;

sometimes we do not. In the latter case, we must accept His goodness by faith.

Sometimes, life experiences cause us to question His goodness. Our foster daughter recently asked, "Why does Jesus let bad things happen to us?" Sometimes, we can only trust God in the circumstances. Joseph's brothers threw him into a pit, Potiphar's wife claimed he tried raping her (a lie), prisoners said they would speak on Joseph's behalf but failed to do so. Joseph ended up in Egypt, separated from his family. Even though he rose to a position of authority in Egypt, the circumstances that led him to that position were far from good. At the conclusion of the story, though, we see Joseph's perspective:

> As for you, you meant evil against me, but God meant it for good in order to bring about this present result, to preserve many people alive. (Gen. 50:20)

No one—neither Joseph nor his brothers—could predict how God would orchestrate those circumstances for their good. We may not see any way that God can arrange our circumstances into anything good. However, the test of His goodness is not our perspective but His character. He alone sees the complete picture, and He alone can orchestrate the outcome. God is faithful!

If God is good and everything God does is good, then God's design for our sexuality must be good as well. Our culture tells us that the biblical view of sex is old-fashioned or narrow-minded. It says we should indulge in sexual practices that feel good. It says that as long as all parties agree, we can enjoy whatever sexual experiences we wish to try. It tells us sex is only something we do with no connection to who we are. Culture tells us *its* view of sex is good and *God's* view is not good. Ask the single person, with no foreseeable option for marriage, "Is God's call for abstinence for you as a single person a good thing?" I suspect many would answer "No!"

However, if we realize God is inherently good and everything He does is good, we can conclude:

1. God is not a "cosmic killjoy" who wants to keep us from enjoying things in life—like sex; and

2. God's design for sex is for our good.

As one writer concludes:

> The fact is, God's rules for sex have nothing to do with keeping anyone from enjoying the best sex, and have everything to do with making sure we do not settle for less than the best. The problem we have with this usually is that we doubt whether we can believe God's holiness is actually more positive than indulging in our passions.[69]

- *God knows everything* (Psalm 139:1-6, 147:5, 1 John 3:20b). God knows every action, thought, intention, and desire; past present or future. Period. Think a minute about what that means. God knows our struggles with purity. He knows when we fail. He knows the dark corners of our heart that we do not reveal to anyone else. Yet He loves us anyway!

- *God is everywhere* (Psalm 139:7-12). Have you ever tried to hide from God? I have! When we think about it, we realize how silly it is. How can we hide from someone who exists *everywhere*??? No matter where I am, God is there with me. We cannot escape God, which means we cannot hide from Him when we sin. If we are in the back room accessing internet porn, God is in the room. But neither can we be anywhere outside the reach of His faithfulness! No matter where or when a temptation may strike, He is there!

---

69 Heimbach, 337.

- *God is our Father* (Matt. 6:26, Gal. 4:6). Someone's relationship with their earthly father influences their view of God as Father. If we had an unhealthy relationship with our earthly father, we likely struggle to think of the Father positively. Perhaps our earthly father was emotionally distant, too strict, physically absent, verbally abusive, or physically abusive. We then often think of God in those same terms. If that is you, let me ask you to try something: Set aside, at least for now, the image of "father" created by your earthly father (as best you can) and see your heavenly Father in light of what the Bible says about Him. I know this is not easy to do. God is the perfect father, and our earthly fathers are imperfect. Pray something to this effect as you try this: "God, let me see you as you are, not tainted through the eyes of my life experiences." Later in this chapter, I provide an exercise that can help us see the full scope of God's character.

As a taste of what God is really like, in one short passage, Paul speaks volumes about God as our Father:

> But when the fullness of the time came, God sent forth His Son, born of a woman, born under the Law, so that He might redeem those who were under the Law, that we might receive the adoption as sons. Because you are sons, God has sent forth the Spirit of His Son into our hearts, crying, "Abba! Father!" Therefore you are no longer a slave, but a son; and if a son, then an heir through God. (Gal. 4:5-7).

First, He sent His Son to redeem us. The significance of redemption came to life for me while visiting Ghana, Africa. While there, I visited the Elmina Castle. The name may sound exotic, but for nearly 400 years, this "castle" served as a holding site for slaves where they endured horrific conditions until their captors shipped them away. A slave entering Elmina had only two options for leaving: through the "door of no return" which led to the slave ships or through death.

In my mind's eye, I pictured a slave standing in the courtyard of the castle, expecting death or worse. I let my imagination run, and instead of seeing this slave endure the fate of every other slave who passed through the castle, I imagined paying the full price for him. But instead of forcing him to serve as my slave, I told him, "You are free. Your life is yours again, and you never need to worry about becoming a slave again. You are free forever." Had this happened, can you imagine the emotions that slave felt? Sadly, we have no record that any such an event occurred in Elmina, but in our lives, it *has* happened. God redeemed us—paid the price in full for us. That is redemption—being set free by the payment of a price on our behalf, no longer slaves to sin, but free in Christ.

He redeemed us to *adopt us as sons and to make us heirs.* God adopted us into His family as His children with all the rights and privileges that come with being His child. The adoption is "through Jesus to Himself" (Eph. 1:5) and is based entirely on what Christ has done for us. God places us fully, legally, and irrevocably into His family the moment we believe (John 1:12). The Father Himself and Jesus both firmly clasp us in their hands (John 10:28-29), so absolutely nothing can change our status as His adopted children.

Even more, He *sent the Spirit into our hearts.* God gives the Spirit to every believer the moment he believes. At that same moment, He seals us and gives us the Spirit as a down payment "of our inheritance, with a view to the redemption of God's own possession" (Eph. 1:14). Sealing guarantees that we belong to God and the down payment guarantees more to come, just as earnest money for a house guarantees the buyer will pay the remainder of the balance owed. Unlike human buyers, God will never renege on his "contract." His resources are unlimited, and He is faithful.

The indwelling Spirit allows us to cry out "Abba, Father." *Abba*, which we can loosely translate "Daddy," is a term of familiarity, closeness, and trust. I saw the meaning of this word one day walking the streets of Old Jerusalem. A man and his very young daughter walked in front of us, but the daughter started lagging behind and became agitated. She yelled out, with a bit of a waver in her voice, "ABBA!!!" He stopped, turned around, knelt on one knee, and without saying a word, opened his arms to her. She ran to him, and he hugged her. I don't know what, if anything, was said between them, but at that moment I could see his love for her and her relief in his arms. As "Abba, Father," we have full access to God anytime and we can ask Him anything, trusting Him to "give what is good to those who ask Him!" (Matt. 7:11).

God is a perfect, loving Father. The best human father pales by comparison.

- *God forgives* (Acts 10:43, Col. 1:14, 2:13, 1 John 1:9). God forgives us on at least two levels: Positional forgiveness and family forgiveness.[70] In the first, we are justified—declared "not guilty"—when we believe in Jesus. (Rom. 5:1). At that moment, God forgives us *all* our sins, past, present, or future; thought or deed; big or little (Col. 2:13). This forgiveness includes *every* sexual sin we have committed or may commit. Moreover, much like the American doctrine of double jeopardy, God will never bring charges against us again because Jesus has paid the price in full (Col. 2:14, 1 John 2:2). God forever guarantees our legal standing before Him. Never again must we seek this forgiveness. We enter into a permanent Father/child relationship with God.

But, we do need "family forgiveness" from God. When we sin, like a disobedient child, our fellowship with God changes. A parent never stops being the biological parent

---

70 For an excellent resource to explore positional forgiveness and family forgiveness or other issues in 1 John (such as confession), see David R. Anderson, *Maximum Joy: 1 John—Relationship or Fellowship?* (NP: Grace Theology Press, 2013).

of their child, no matter how that child misbehaves. They discipline him; they may be angry with him, the child may be angry at the parents. Even though the child never stops being the child of the parents, the fellowship between them changes. If I took my dad's car without permission, then hit a telephone pole with it, I doubt he would be smiling and talking about last night's baseball game with me. He would still love me (no parent in a healthy home stops loving the child), but how that love acts changes. The parent now acts as the disciplinarian. In a healthy home, this discipline is an act of love for my good. Even painful discipline!

The same thing happens with our relationship with God when we sin. God makes us His children forever the moment we believe. When we sin, He does not "unadopt" us. That status with Him *never* changes. He is forever our Father; we are forever His child. However, when we sin, our family dynamics with Him change. Since He is a perfect Father, we never worry about whether he will stop loving us, but what that love looks like changes. When we sin, we place ourselves in a position deserving discipline *from the hand of a loving Father who desires to restore us* (Heb. 12:4-11).

How do we experience family forgiveness with God? By confessing the sins we committed (1 John 1:9). When we do this, He is "faith and righteous to forgive us our sins and to cleanse us from all unrighteousness." He grants us family forgiveness. We might still experience consequences, but "the air is cleared" between us. Chapter Eleven addresses this process more fully.

- *God is patient* (Psalm 103:8, Rom. 2:4). Biblical patience is "a God-exercised, or God-given, restraint in face of opposition or oppression."[71] He is "slow to anger." God does not condone

---

71 D. R. W. Wood, *New Bible Dictionary* (Downers Grove, IL: InterVarsity Press, 1996), s.v. "patience."

sin nor does He take it lightly, but He gives His people opportunities to deal with their sin. God often responds more slowly than we think He ought. We sometimes expect God to react instantly when we sin, but He is slow to anger with us as well.

God is faithful, holy, loving, good, forgiving; He lives everywhere, knows everything, and is our Father. He has redeemed us, adopted us, given us the Holy Spirit, made us heirs, and allows us to approach Him as "Abba, Father!" All this is just scratching the surface. He is a great God! Rick Warren summarizes well:

The closer you live to God, the smaller everything else appears.[72]

God's inherent *glory is what he possesses because he is God. It is his nature. We cannot add anything to his glory . . . But we are commanded to* recognize *his glory,* honor *his glory,* declare *his glory,* praise *his glory,* reflect *his glory, and* live *for his glory. Why? Because God deserves it!*[73]

Do you want to know more about God? Try this exercise: [74]

1. Read through the Psalms, with some means for taking notes while you read. If reading all the Psalms seems overwhelming, take bite-size pieces, for example, reading Psalm 139, Psalm 145, and Psalm 121.

2. Each time you see a statement about God, highlight it (underline it in your Bible, write it down, whatever method works).

---

72 Rick Warren, *The Purpose Driven Life* (Grand Rapids, MI: Zondervan, 2002), 37.

73 Ibid., 54 (emphasis his).

74 Special thanks to my seminary professor, Dr. Norm Wakefield, who gave this as a class assignment. It was perhaps the most meaningful and thought-provoking assignment in my seminary career.

3. Periodically, make a list of your observations.

4. Use this list to meditate on the character of God. Ask questions. What does this mean? What does it look like in life? Have I seen this attribute in action?

5. Use this list to thank God for who He is and for His character.

Here is one verse as an example. Psalm 145:8 says "The Lord is *gracious* and *merciful; Slow to anger* and *great in lovingkindness."* I have highlighted what it says about God (not every verse will have as many statements as this verse; some might have none). My notes would include each of these four attributes. From this list of attributes, I might decide to focus on God's graciousness. I thank Him that He is gracious. I reflect on what "grace" means—receiving what we do not deserve for everything in life. I thank Him that He saves us by His grace. And on and on. I hope you get the idea!

Do not rush through the exercise. Let the words of Scripture sink into your heart and mind.

Technically, God's *power* is another dimension of His person. However, because of the strength of sexual temptation and the flesh, I list His power as a separate aspect of the foundation. I have heard too many men say something like, "The temptation was too strong. I just couldn't help myself." Or, "I have a strong sex drive. I can't resist a natural response!"

The Bible tells us repeatedly that nothing is impossible with God. His power knows no limits. God is called "the Lord God Almighty" (Rev. 4:8). Jeremiah proclaimed, "Ah Lord God! Behold, You have made the heavens and the earth by Your great power and by Your outstretched arm! *Nothing is too difficult for You"* (Jer. 32:17). He created the universe, and He holds it together; He raised Jesus from the dead; He gives life to us when we are spiritually dead, and He will one day decisively defeat every one of His enemies.

He provides us with a direct connection to this power. Here is how: "But I say, walk by the Spirit, and you will not carry out the desire of the flesh" (Gal. 5:16). At the risk of stating the obvious, the passage does not say "you *probably* won't carry out the desire of the flesh" or "you *might not* carry out the deed of the flesh." The Greek emphatically says, "You *will not* carry out the desire of the flesh." We could loosely paraphrase it as "you will no way, no how, give in to sexual temptations." Our faithful God promised that if we walk in the Spirit, we will not carry out the desire of the flesh. The Spirit is stronger than the flesh, than the world, than the devil (1 John 4:4), *stronger than the power of any sexual temptation*! Now *that is* power!

The bottom line: God's power, not our own, is the key to experience ongoing purity.

Why is this so important? We can quote the verse, yet, when faced with the power of our flesh pulling us in the wrong direction, we become "practical atheists." I realize this sounds bad. Here is what it means: We act as if the promise does not exist. However, the fact that we *act* as if the power is not there does not mean the power is not there in reality. The problem lies in living out the promise. Later, we will see how this works (Chapter Six), but for now, be aware that *God's* power provides us the power for success.

His person should motivate us towards purity; His power means we have the ability to experience purity; and in His provisions, we have *everything* we need to experience purity:

> Grace and peace be multiplied to you in the knowledge of God and of Jesus our Lord; seeing that His divine power *has granted to us everything pertaining to life and godliness*, through the true knowledge of Him who called us by His own glory and excellence. (2 Pet 1:2-3)

What has God given us? As you read the next few pages, you might well think, "Duh! I know that!" Sometimes, though, reminders help. So here goes! Some of God's provisions on our behalf include:

The Bible: It is amazing how God provided His Word for us. He worked in and through the lives of dozens of people over hundreds of years to pen His words without error (We call this the doctrine of inspiration and inerrancy). As we unfold its pages, we see the truth about God, about ourselves, and about what He has done. It tells us

what to do, how to do it, and why we should do it. If we believe the
Bible is God's Word, then we know its words accurately reflect God's
character. Further, we should conclude that the principles and promises
it contains are for our good.

The Holy Spirit: As we have already seen, the Spirit indwells *every*
believer the moment he or she believes (Rom. 8:9, 1 Cor. 12:13).
The Spirit secures us in Christ and provides the "power source" for
successful Christian living in every area of life, including sexual purity.

His promises: Because God is faithful, He guarantees the promises
He gives us in His Word! When he says, "How can a young man keep
his way pure? By keeping it according to Your word" (Psalm 119:9),
we know purity is possible—it is a promise. When Jesus said, "If you
continue in My word . . . you will know the truth, and the truth will
make you free" (John 8:31-32), we know freedom is possible, including
freedom from the grip of sexual sin—it is a promise. When He says
no temptation is too strong and that He will provide a way of escape,
we can trust that *no* sexual temptation is too strong—it is a promise.
When He says He will never leave us or forsake us, we know He will
never leave us—it is a promise. When He says we will not carry out the
deeds of the flesh when we walk in the Spirit, we can believe we do not
need to yield to the flesh- it is a promise. And where do we discover
these incredible promises? In His Word.

Other believers: God never designed Christians to live independently
of one another. The New Testament frequently gives commands about
serving one another, commands like:

> Brethren, even if anyone is caught in any trespass, you who are
> spiritual, restore such a one in a spirit of gentleness; each one
> looking to yourself, so that you too will not be tempted. Bear
> one another's burdens, and thereby fulfill the law of Christ. (Gal.
> 6:1-2)

> Therefore I, the prisoner of the Lord, implore you to walk in
> a manner worthy of the calling with which you have been
> called, with all humility and gentleness, with patience, showing
> tolerance for one another in love. (Eph. 4:1-2)

Therefore, confess your sins to one another, and pray for one another so that you may be healed. The effective prayer of a righteous man can accomplish much. (James 5:16)

For this is the message which you have heard from the beginning, that we should love one another. (1 John 3:11)

God gave us one another to encourage and help us in our lives. Granted, believers do not always live this way, but that does not change the fact that God designed us this way. God designed the church, which consists of believers everywhere, to be a people that serve one another for their mutual good.

Our Identity in Christ: I was one of two pastors in a church in Louisiana. When I walked into the office one day, I let Tim know I was there by hollering, "Just me!" Tim decided to give me a bad time and informed me "You are so much more than 'just me.' You are a new creature in Christ. You belong to the family of God! You're not just a 'just me.'" The next day, lesson learned, I walked into the office and loudly proclaimed, "It is I! A child of the King!"

The "deep down" answer to the question "who am I?" reflects how we see ourselves. I can give a verbal answer, but that answer may not tell the whole story. Like most men, if someone asks me about myself, I would probably begin talking about my job, my family, and maybe my hobbies. Most men say something about what they do. "I am a pastor; I'm married with five kids (three children plus two daughters-in-law) and seven grandchildren. I am a foster parent. I love to hunt and fish." Those answers, although true, do not say much about how I see myself. Deep down, we often *think* about our adequacy as a person. We tell ourselves things like, "I'm not a very good teacher" or "I'm a lousy athlete" or "I really don't matter much at all" or "I'm a failure." Who we think we are affects how we live.

For the Christian, who we are has nothing to do with what we do or what we think of ourselves. When I became a believer, God gave me a new identity, but my flesh did not disappear. Wouldn't it make life easier if we had neither the desire nor capacity to sin?

> In bestowing this gift (our new heart) at our conversion, God
> doesn't remove our old heart. When we trust Christ for salvation,
> our sinful nature is not *removed* but *offset*.[75]

This view recognizes that God fundamentally changes who we are
when we believe in Christ, yet, acknowledges the biblical view that
our flesh remains. Paul describes himself some thirty years after his
conversion: "I *am* (present tense) the foremost of sinners" (1 Tim.
1:15). I once heard a line in a song someone sang at church: "I'm just a
sinner saved by grace!" It is true that I *am* a sinner saved by grace, but
I am not *just* a sinner saved by grace. I am *much more* because of what
Christ did for me. My core identity—the "real me," so to speak—is not
the "me" limited and driven by the flesh, nor the "me" that I see when I
evaluate myself incorrectly, but the "me" that I am in Christ.

So, who am I? Here's a start: I am a child of God; a new creation in
Christ; a saint by calling; blessed with every spiritual blessing; sealed
in Him by the Holy Spirit; once spiritually dead but now alive in Him;
loved completely by God; forgiven of every transgression; justified by
faith; no longer an enemy of God; a priest of God; a man called out
of darkness into light; a recipient of God's mercy; no longer a slave to
sin.[76] I could add more, but even this incomplete list gives you an idea
about the real me! If you have believed in Jesus for eternal life, this
describes the real you as well. And this description is not based on my
opinion or your opinion, but on the truthfulness of God's Word. That's
good news! What the Bible says about our identity is true because
God's Word says so, but deep down, do we believe it? When God tells
us to live a sexually pure life, He wants us to live like who we are in
Christ, His children.

Some of the terms describing the "real me" need some explanation.
We could spend time on each of them, but we will only look at four: I

---

75 Dwight Edwards, *Revolution Within* (Colorado Springs: WaterBrook Press,
   2001), 54.

76 See, in order, 2 Cor. 5:17, John 1:12, 1 Cor. 1:2, Eph. 1:3, Eph. 1:13, Eph. 2:4-5,
   Eph. 5:25, Col. 2:13, Rom. 5:1, 1 Pet. 2:9-10, and Romans 6:5-7.

am justified by faith, I am a saint by calling, I am loved completely by God, and I am no longer a slave to sin.

I am justified by faith (Rom. 3:21-28, Gal. 2:16). Justification is "a forensic term, denoting a judicial act of administering the law—in this case, by declaring a verdict of acquittal, and so excluding all possibility of condemnation. Justification thus settles the legal status of the person justified."[77] Too technical? Here is the picture: God, as sovereign judge, bangs the gavel and says, "You believed in my Son for eternal life. Therefore, you are not guilty. I declare you righteous!" To be justified means I am forever declared "not guilty." I am forever declared righteous, based on what Jesus did on our behalf. Justification *permanently* changes our legal standing before God. *That* is good news!!!

Have you believed in Jesus as the one who died for your sins, the one God raised from the dead, and the one who gives you eternal life? If not, what is holding you back from doing so now? You do not need to do anything except believe. The rest is God's grace—His free gift to you.

I am a saint: The New Testament repeatedly calls believers "saints." We often think of saints as those specially recognized for their holiness or their virtue. That is not what the Bible means by "saint." The Bible calls every believer a saint, even those who are not living a healthy Christian life. The church at Corinth struggled with a host of problems, issues like quarreling, divisiveness, abusing the Lord's supper, immorality by some and responding incorrectly to that immorality by others. Hardly what one would call a model church! In fact, Paul said he could not speak to these brethren "as to spiritual men, but as to men of flesh, as to infants in Christ" (1 Cor. 3:1). These same believers are addressed as "those who have been sanctified in Christ Jesus, *saints* by calling" (1 Cor. 1:2).

So what is a saint? The New Testament word for "saint" is the same word translated "holy." In fact, some translations use the phrase "holy ones" instead of "saint." It means God sees us as holy—set apart—

---

77 Walter A. Elwell, ed., *Evangelical Dictionary of Theology* (Grand Rapids: MI: Baker Book House, 1984), s.v. "Justification."

because of our identity with Christ. Positionally, we are "holy." We *cannot earn* the title "saint." We are saints because of what Christ has done for us. God, the holy one, sets us apart as "saints" the moment we believe and only then commands us to live holy lives.

I am loved completely by God (Rom. 8:31-35, 38-39). I do not think we can overemphasize God's love for His children. I recently heard a man say he used to see God as a "scowling, frowning super cop out to stop anyone from having a good time." But God is a loving father, not a cosmic killjoy. He loves us more than we can imagine! In this passage in Romans, Paul asks four questions about our standing before God:

1. If God is for us, who is against us?

2. Who will bring a charge against God's elect?

3. Who is the one who condemns?

4. Who will separate us from the love of Christ?

The implied answer to the first three questions is, "No one that counts!" Sure, some (including the devil and his minions) are against us, some will bring charges against us, and some will try to condemn us. Sometimes we condemn ourselves! However, none of these has any viability in light of Christ's work on our behalf. The charges, the accusations, the condemnation mean nothing to God because of what Christ has done on our behalf.

Then, the fourth question wonders about the extent of God's love for us. Look at the answer:

Will tribulation, or distress, or persecution, or famine, or nakedness, or peril, or sword? . . . For I am convinced that neither death, nor life, nor angels, nor principalities, nor things present, nor things to come, nor powers, nor height, nor depth, nor any other created thing, will be able to separate us from the love of God, which is in Christ Jesus our Lord."

Did you catch the last phrase? *Nothing* can "separate us from the love of God." That includes me—I cannot separate myself from His love. And *it includes the sexual sin with which I struggle.* Absolutely nothing can separate me from God's love for me. Sin is serious, but it never, ever causes God to cease loving us. Never. His love is unconditional and unlimited.

What does this love look like when we sin? It does not sweep our sin under the rug as if nothing happened. God's love sent Jesus to die for our sin so that Jesus would pay in full the legal penalty for sin. Our position before God is that of one completely forgiven of all their sins (Col. 2:13). However, as a loving Father, God will not ignore sin in our life. God will discipline us. Unlike the "scowling, frowning super cop out to stop anyone from having a good time," God disciplines us as a loving Father for our good:

FOR THOSE WHOM THE LORD LOVES HE DISCIPLINES, AND HE SCOURGES EVERY SON WHOM HE RECEIVES. It is for discipline that you endure; God deals with you as with sons; for what son is there whom his father does not discipline? . . . For they disciplined us for a short time as seemed best to them, but He disciplines us for our good, so that we may share His holiness. (Heb. 12:6-7, 11)

He wants us to live rightly, He wants us to glorify Him, and He wants us to experience "life abundantly." As a loving, perfect Father, He will do what He needs to do to train us and move us toward those good goals. Our sin could result in *discipline* from God, but it will never *separate* us from His love. We may think, "What I did is so bad, God cannot love me." Sadly, too many buy this lie! The truth is, God loves us unconditionally as His children. Once I believe in Jesus and receive eternal life, He will *never* cease loving me.

I am no longer a slave to sin as my master (Rom 6:5-7, 11-14). Not only am I a legally free man forever, I am also no longer under a legal obligation to sin as my day-to-day master. You may well be thinking at this point, "Yeah, right . . . sounds good, but it doesn't work. Sin gets the better of me far too often!" Later, we'll see how to put this principle into action, but for now realize that because of our identity with Jesus' death, burial, and resurrection, the legal reign sin had as master over us is null and void.

This description of our identity in Christ is far from exhaustive, but I hope you see the point. God fundamentally changes our identity—who we are at our very core—when we become a Christian. You can describe me as a father, a husband, a friend, a writer, a pastor, a sports fan, and many other things. However, all these descriptions are secondary to who I am at my core. If I misidentify the core, the "real me," chances are I will not be the father or husband that I could be. In the realm of sexual purity, if I misidentify the "real me," I might very well conclude that sexual temptation simply has more power than it does, and I then fail to experience purity the way God desires. When I grasp my real identity in Christ, every aspect of my life takes on a different—and better—meaning.

It is appropriate here to address a critical issue with which many people struggle. That issue is *shame*. It is particularly pertinent to the issue of sexual purity. What is "shame?" It is an unhealthy view of oneself, a view contrary to our true identity in Christ. Guilt says, "I did something wrong." Shame says, "There is something wrong with me." It is a "feeling of being inwardly flawed—of not measuring up."[78] It says, "I am a mistake."[79] Shame may lead to the unbiblical conclusions, "God can't possibly love me," or "Why should God forgive me again? I've already confessed this a million times." I once met a woman who concluded God could not love her because she was "damaged goods." Her feelings resulted from a brother sexually abusing her for years and from parents supporting him rather than protecting her. She could not see God's love for her. Instead, she saw Him as she *imagined* He saw her—damaged beyond love.

Shame starts with two true premises but draws an incorrect, unhealthy conclusion from those premises. The first true premise is:

---

78 Alan D. Wright, *Free Yourself, Be Yourself: Find the Power to Escape Your Past*, (Colorado Springs, CO: Multnomah Press, 2010), 17. This book and related resources are helpful in understanding and overcoming shame. The title is misleading in that the book is not a self-help book, but rather addresses a biblical response to shame. It was previously published as *Shame Off You*. See www.sharingthelight.org.

79 Ibid., 85.

We all want to be loved and accepted. The second true premise is: We are flawed. The Bible makes that clear, "For all have sinned and fall short of the glory of God" (Rom. 3:23). Unfortunately, some of us (most of us?) then conclude that, because I am flawed, I am inadequate, unlovable, and not worthy of love. Many painful life experiences feed this painful conclusion, such as:

- Blaming ourselves for something bad (e.g., kids blaming themselves for the parent's divorce)

- Being the target of harsh words from others (verbal abuse, bullying)

- Experiencing abuse (sexual, physical, emotional)

- Being neglected as a child ("There must be something wrong with me if they ignore me")

- Evaluating ourselves incorrectly (I was not naturally athletic, but many of the popular kids were, so, growing up, I thought I needed to be athletic to be okay)

- Living with a dysfunctional family

These wounds are deeper than mere physical wounds; they scar our emotions and self-perception. "I've never met anyone who had no inner pain. What's your hidden hornet? Deep loneliness? Unhealed emotional wounds? Repeated rejections? An alcoholic dad?"[80] Most of us try to hide or numb the shame, an approach which is counterproductive. Neither hiding nor numbing leads to a better, fuller life. In relationships with others, especially in the context of marriage, we hide our shame because we fear rejection. The result? Diminished intimacy, shallower friendships. In our relationship with God, shame pushes us away from Him (much as Adam and Eve hid from Him, Gen. 3:8) instead of driving us towards Him.[81] The result?

---

80 Ibid., 62. The image of the hornet sting is a metaphor for whatever it is that "stings" us in life.

81 The shame Adam experienced differed from the shame we experience because he started from a sinless (unflawed) position and experienced unhindered

Diminished intimacy with God. Some cover their shame by becoming overachieving perfectionists to "prove" they are not a mistake. Some "self-medicate" to numb the inner ache through drugs, alcohol, acting out sexually and similar means.

> I spoke softly, 'I think shame hasn't helped you stop looking at pornography—I think shame is the reason you're tempted toward it in the first place. The pressure of feeling like you've got to do better in order to be accepted is causing the hidden anxiety in your soul. It's that anxiety that you're numbing with the fantasy of pornography. If you don't measure up, that you aren't the full man that you know you are supposed to be, then you resort to two-dimensional women in a magazine or on a web page. Those nameless women always accept you. There is no risk of rejection from them. Shame isn't the cure for pornography addiction—it's the root of it.'[82]

Hiding or numbing the shame does not fix anything. In fact, it may well lead to deeper shame. The cure for shame is to see ourselves as God sees us—that is, to see ourselves as who we are in Christ! It starts by taking a different turn after the realization that we are, in fact, flawed. Instead of believing we are less loved and inadequate, the better approach believes that God *does* love us unconditionally and in Him we are complete; we are adequate by His grace; we are not a mistake.

God does not love us because we are lovable or because we are less flawed than others. He loves us by His choice, despite any and all sins we have committed. When we see ourselves less through the eyes of shame and more through the eyes of grace, we are less prone to use sexual activity as a means of hiding or numbing that shame. It

---

fellowship with God. His guilt required confession, but his actions indicate that he experienced shame in addition to guilt. Before the fall, he was "naked and not ashamed" (Gen. 2:25). Now, he covered his nakedness (Gen. 3:10), hid from God (Gen. 3:8), and blamed others—including God—for his actions (Gen. 3:12). Thus, when he sinned, both guilt and shame entered the world.

82 Ibid., 78.

means playing the tape of God's Word in our minds when the tape of our shame tries to get our attention. We can start by meditating on principles like these:

- For God so loved *me* that He gave His only begotten Son, that if *I* believe in Him, *I* shall not perish, but have eternal life. (John 3:16)

- For while *I* was still helpless, at the right time Christ died for ungodly *me*. (Rom. 5:6)

- But God demonstrates His own love toward *me*, in that while *I* was yet a sinner, Christ died for *me*. (Rom. 5:8)

- For while *I* was an enemy, *I* was reconciled to God through the death of His Son (Rom. 5:8a)

- *I* love because He first loved *me*. (1 John 4:19)[83]

Do you see it? God loves each one of us, a love initiated by Him, independent of our character. So, we want to be loved and accepted, we are flawed, but God loves us unconditionally, and thus shame need not hold us! We are free to become the people God desires us to be. The changes in our thinking, the cure of the shame, will likely not come overnight, but the more fully we realize who we are in Christ, the less power the lying voice of shame has in our lives. And we don't need to numb our pain by seeking temporary pleasure through acting out sexually.

The foundation upon which we build our purity—God's person, power, and provisions—is *unconditional and unchanging*. Whether we ever think about them or apply them is, in one sense, immaterial. Nothing we do changes the unchanging character of God. Nothing we do renders the power of God powerless. No matter how we live, we can never change the core identity of who we are in Christ. Understanding the foundation helps us define a goal for purity that aligns with His

---

83 In each case, the pronouns in the Scripture listed were changed to personalize it. For example, in John 3:16, "God so loved the world" was modified to "God so loved *me*," recognizing that I am part of the world. It changes the verse from being abstract ("the world") to showing how God sees each of us.

character, motivates us to live a life that reflects who we are as children of God, and helps us understand the resources God has given us to experience purity. The rest of the book describes the frame of the house, connecting the foundation to our lives so we can achieve the purity we desire!

CHAPTER SIX

FOLLOW THE LEADER

Principle #1: Connect regularly with God

I start every morning with a cup of coffee before I head to the office. One typical Monday morning, I put in a new filter, carefully measured out three scoops of grounds, poured water into the coffee maker, and pressed "on." I left the kitchen to get ready for work, anticipating when I returned the aroma of freshly brewed coffee. Instead, I smelled nothing. It turns out I failed to plug in the pot, and nothing happened! Many things in our world cannot work without power. How many times do Christians try to live their lives without relying on the power God gives us? We live unplugged—and defeated.

Keep in mind our power source far surpasses mere electricity. Ultimately, it is God Himself in the person of the Holy Spirit—infinite, personal, all-powerful, forever present, indwelling. He empowers us to live as God wants us to live, to become who God desires us to be in Christ, to say "no" to sin. But it's not automatic. Doesn't it seem foolish to try to live our Christian life on our own without "plugging in?"

This chapter addresses three keys to connect the power of God with our sexual purity: Taking in the Word of God, communicating with

God in prayer, and obeying God by walking in the Spirit.[84] These three practices are neither rituals that automatically result in growth and purity, nor are they measures of our spirituality. Instead, they are *tools*.

I recently helped a group of high school students prepare for a statewide mathematics competition. Only three students could participate on the team, so all the students worked hard to learn the math, hoping to make the team. But once on the team, their motives for studying changed. They no longer worried about *making* the team. Instead, they worked hard because they were *on* the team. The studying served as a *tool* to mold them into the best math students possible for the competition.

We join God's family ("the team") the moment we believe in Jesus for eternal life. Once in the family, our position is secure. We are secure in Christ because of what He has done for us. Practices such as reading the Bible and prayer are not ends in themselves; instead, they equip us for living and for experiencing a close relationship with God. John Ortberg captures the idea well:

> There is an immense difference between *training* to do something and *trying* to do something . . . For much of my life, when I heard messages about following Jesus, I thought in terms of trying hard to be like him. So after hearing (or preaching, for that matter) a sermon on patience Sunday morning, I would wake up Monday morning determined to be a more patient person . . . it generally didn't work any better than trying hard to run a marathon for which I had not trained. I would end up exhausted and defeated . . . Spiritual transformation is not a matter of training harder but training wisely . . . Respecting the distinction between training and merely trying is the key to transformation in every area of life.[85]

---

84 Of course, living out the Christian life and growing in our relationship with God involves more than these three practices. These three are the core essentials if we wish to experience purity.

85 John Ortberg, *The Life You've Always Wanted* (Grand Rapids, MI: Zondervan Publishing House, 1997), 47-48.

He wraps up the idea with these wise words: "Our primary task is not to calculate how many verses of Scripture we read or how many minutes we spend in prayer. Our task is to use these activities to create opportunities for God to work."[86] The three practices in this chapter are a *means* to an end, not the *ends* themselves. God uses them to change us from the inside out and to reveal Himself to us; they are tools.

Bible Intake (reading, memorizing, meditating). "How can a young man keep his way pure? By keeping it *according to Your word*" (Psalm 119:9. The Bible equips us for every good work, including our purity:

All Scripture is inspired by God and profitable for teaching [doctrine, content], for reproof [revealing error in thought or practice], for correction [correcting the error], for training in righteousness [right living]; so that the man of God may be adequate, equipped for every good work. (2 Tim. 3:16-17).

The Scriptures teach us about:

- God's person and work.
- The provisions God has given us.
- Sin (including sexual sin) and its seriousness.
- Our true identity as Christians.
- Instructions for living righteously.
- God's promises to and for us.
- The benefits of following Him.
- The history of what God has done and will do.

Look at these two key verses related to purity:

No temptation has overtaken you but such as is common to man; (*who we are*) and God is faithful, (*God's person*) who will

---

86 Ibid., 57.

not allow you to be tempted beyond what you are able, (*God's promises*) but with the temptation will provide the way of escape also (*the provisions God has given us*) so that you will be able to endure it. (*the benefits of following Him*).[87]

Flee immorality (*instructions for living righteously*). Every other sin that a man commits is outside the body, but the immoral man sins against his own body (*sin and its seriousness*). Or do you not know that your body is a temple of the Holy Spirit who is in you (*our true identity as Christians*), whom you have from God (*the provisions God has given us*), and that you are not your own? For you have been bought with a price (*our true identity as Christians*): therefore glorify God in your body (*instructions for living righteously*).[88]

I suspect most readers at this point would agree that the Bible is important. And I'm sure you have noticed this book relies heavily on the Scriptures. The problem many of us face is actually *reading* it! Why is it so difficult to read consistently, let alone memorize or meditate on what it says? We face four possible obstacles to reading (you may think of others).

The first obstacle is legitimate guilt (knowing we sinned), which may lead to shame.[89] The person indulging his flesh and actively involved in some sin such as accessing internet porn *knows* what he is doing is wrong. I remember as a youngster taking money from where my parents kept spare change, walking to the corner store, and buying baseball cards. I knew I was wrong, so the last people I wanted to see were my mom or dad. I felt guilty—legitimately. When we sin, we avoid the Bible exactly because we want to avoid being further convicted ("reproof"). When we choose this route, however, we *miss* the healing

---

87 1 Corinthians 10:13.

88 1 Corinthians 6:18-20.

89 Dealing with shame was addressed in Chapter Five; dealing with guilt will be addressed in Chapter Eleven.

power of God's word (correction and training in righteousness). Look at David's example after his sexual sin with Bathsheba:

> How blessed is he whose transgression is *forgiven*,
> Whose sin is *covered*!
> How blessed is the man to whom the Lord *does not impute iniquity*,
> And in whose spirit there is no deceit!
> When I kept silent about my sin, my body wasted away
> Through my groaning all day long.
> For day and night Your hand was heavy upon me;
> My vitality was drained away as with the fever heat of summer.
> I acknowledged my sin to You,
> And my iniquity I did not hide;
> I said, "I will confess my transgressions to the Lord";
> And *You forgave the guilt of my sin.*
> Therefore, let everyone who is godly pray to You in a time when You
>   may be found;
> Surely in a flood of great waters they will not reach him.
> You are my hiding place; You preserve me from trouble;
> You surround me with songs of deliverance. (Psalm 32:1-7, emphasis
>   added)

When David kept silent about his sin, he was miserable. When he confessed his sin, he experienced forgiveness! When our guilt and shame keep us from reading the Scriptures, we may miss the very words we need to hear to deal with our sin and guilt.

Shame goes a step further than guilt. True guilt, recognizing that we sinned, is an appropriate response when we sin. Shame, as we saw in the last chapter, goes beyond saying "I failed" and says "I'm a failure." Both will keep us out of God's Word, and both may drive us *towards* sexual sin to medicate the emotional pain—a common, yet counterproductive, response.

A second obstacle is, the Bible is sometimes difficult to understand. The problem may be the general readability of the translation, or it may be the complexity of a particular passage or topic. After all, even Peter said Paul is sometimes hard to understand (2 Pet. 3:15-16)!

Any book can be evaluated for its readability, the results reported as a "grade level readability." The average reading level of American adults is 7th to 8th-grade level.[90] Bibles are evaluated on the same basis.[91] Universally, The King James Version is listed as the most difficult to read, but the New American Standard is not far behind. The New King James Version and the New International Version both score near the 8th-grade reading level. Some versions (many of which are paraphrases) are even easier to read. If you find the language confusing in the version you are using, investigate some of the other versions. I'd recommend you talk with a pastor or a Bible bookstore about the pros and cons of the various versions. If you read poorly or just don't like reading (regardless of the translation), investigate audio versions of the Bible.

Sometimes the passage itself is difficult to understand or is confusing, no matter the translation used. I have been a believer for over 40 years, I have graduated from seminary, I have served as a pastor for nearly twenty years, I've taught Bible school and seminary courses, and I *still* find some passages difficult to understand! But I understand far more than that first day when my girlfriend (who later became my wife) and I both believed in Jesus for our salvation. The key to growing from that day until now was not my seminary education (although that accelerated the process), but rather *perseverance*. I kept reading even when I was in a tough passage; I attended churches committed to teaching the content and the application of the Bible; I sought help

---

90 http://www.clearlanguagegroup.com/readability/, accessed 11/29/2016. Such scales do not measure how well people comprehend the material and do not reflect the education level of the reader. They measure the difficulty of the text based on several criteria.

91 Since no standard method exists for this measurement, different sources may give different numbers for each translation. However, any source is helpful for relative comparisons, version vs. version, such as http://notjustanother book.com/biblecomparison.htm (accessed June 26, 2017). This resource says the reading level of the KJV is 13th grade; the NASB 11th grade, NKJV 9th grade, and NIV 8th grade.

from commentaries or pastors to help find answers. You, too, can understand more and more of the Bible if you keep pressing on![92]

The third and fourth obstacles to reading are perhaps the most significant. The third obstacle is *choosing* to read. Some days, I simply don't feel like reading the Bible. Be honest—you have those days, too! I know of no sure-fire way to overcome this obstacle other than making a choice to read regardless of what we want at the moment. We do this regularly in other areas of life: I don't always want to go to work, but I make the choice to do so. Making this decision is much like training for the 10K race I ran. Some days, I simply did *not* want to run as scheduled. I knew, however, that not running would hurt my ability to race later, so I put on my running shoes and started running. So choose to read on those days you don't want to, even if it's only a short passage. Train by reading—it makes a real difference.

The fourth and final obstacle is the nature of the Bible itself. I am an avid reader, usually working through more than one book at a time. I've noticed it is easy to read a chapter in a novel or a history book or even a book *about* the Bible, yet reading the Bible feels like a major undertaking. Why the difference? Because there is a spiritual battle going on behind the scenes. Our spiritual enemies—the world, the flesh, and the devil—push against us reading God's Word. Our "struggle is not against flesh and blood, but against the rulers, against the powers, against the world forces of this darkness, against the spiritual forces of wickedness in the heavenly places" (Eph. 6:12). Don't be surprised when reading the Bible feels like a battle because it is!

Don't let the obstacles win. Press on and read. Here are a few hints to help read the Bible more effectively:[93]

---

92 It's helpful to develop the habit of reading the Scripture regularly. Having said that, we need to guard against it becoming a legalistic requirement (I must have quiet time six days a week) or allowing shame to gain a foothold if we get out of the habit.

93 These are by necessity very broad ideas. To learn more, ask your pastor or another church leader to teach a Bible Study Methods class, to teach you one-on-one how to read more effectively, or to recommend a good resource to help you learn how to study the Bible. I recommend *Living By the Book* (Howard G. Hendricks and William D. Hendricks, *Living By the Book: The Art and Science*

- Use a Bible you can mark up. Highlight key verses or phrases as you read.

- Begin with that which is familiar or easier rather than the more difficult. I'd suggest starting with the Psalms or John but leave Revelation or Hebrews for later reading!

- If you are not in the habit of reading, start with bite size pieces, such as a single chapter or even just a few verses.

- The three most important words in effective reading are context, context, and context. Context is especially important when looking at individual verses or short sections. What does the author say before and after the verses? Where in the history of what Scripture reveals does the passage fit (e.g., is it during the period of the law? After the resurrection? Before or after the nation of Israel splits into two nations?).

- Take notes as you read.

- Write down the questions that pop up in your head as you read. Try to avoid being distracted by these questions! Don't ignore them; come back to them at another time.

- Ask the question, "What did the author mean when he wrote to the original audience?"

- After answering, ask the question, "How does that initial intent translate into my life?"

- Meditate on key verses you read. "Meditate" means "think about." For example, reflect on the command "flee immorality." What does it mean? How can I do this in my world? Meditation slows us down enough to process what we have read.

Of course, not everything you read in the Bible pertains directly to sexual purity. But as you develop the habit of reading, you'll find that

---

of *Reading the Bible*, revised and updated, [Chicago: Moody Publishers, 1991, 2007]).

it can help you better understand God, His plans in general, and the specific instructions for life. Long term "success" in any area of life as a believer—including experiencing purity—requires taking in God's Word regularly.

The second key is prayer. In simple terms, prayer is talking with God. The Bible contains examples of prayer, principles for prayer, and commands to pray. Why? First, God is a *personal* God. We are his children; He is our Father. To connect with any person, we must talk and listen. Prayer is the "talking" part of that process. He is our "Abba, Father" (Rom. 8:15, Gal. 4:6) and we have access to the throne of God (Heb. 4:16). Therefore we are free to talk to Him about *anything*—even our sexual struggles! Look at the Psalms: We find words of praise, thanksgiving, grief, sadness, confession, anger, confusion, and many other emotions. Not only are we free to talk to Him about anything, we are also free to talk to Him about everything! By *not* talking to Him, we aren't hiding a single thing from Him. I can hide details of my thoughts and feelings from my wife, my children, and my friends, but I *cannot* hide a single detail from Him. He knows everything about my life—including my sexual failures—and He never cuts me out of His family. He knows everything about us *anyway*, so why not talk to Him?

Another reason to pray is simply the reality that God is God! I know this sounds obvious; maybe even trite. But the fact remains that the one we pray to is the God of the universe! We are the creatures; He is the creator. We are dependent; He is independent. We are finite; He is infinite. We are imperfect; He is perfect. It makes sense that we acknowledge Him in praise and thanksgiving. It makes sense we acknowledge our failings (sin) to Him. And it makes sense we ask Him for the things we need.

How does prayer connect with sexual purity? Here are eight ways:

- Confessing when we fail (1 John 1:9).
- Helping us focus on "things above" (Col. 3:1-2, 17).
- Asking for the promised "way of escape" (1 Cor. 10:13).
- Acknowledging our weakness.
- Expressing faith in Him.

- Going to him in a time of need (Heb. 4:16).
- Giving thanks for His provisions.
- Praising Him for victory.

This third key is the most critical tool in the entire book. We *cannot* consistently overcome the flesh by the flesh; the means of experiencing biblical purity does not come from our effort. Too often, we are left with the impression that if *I* just _____ (you fill in the blank), then *I* will experience purity. The Christian life doesn't work that way. We are not the first people who tried this faulty approach:

> This is the only thing I want to find out from you: did you receive the Spirit by the works of the Law, or by hearing with faith? Are you so foolish? Having begun by the Spirit, are you now being perfected by the flesh? (Gal. 3:2-3)

Flesh cannot defeat flesh; my efforts alone cannot produce godliness; I cannot consistently weather the storms of temptation on my own. It just doesn't work!

> When we come against the flesh in our own strength, it is only a matter of time until all our energy is depleted . . . If the flesh controls our mind, emotions, and will, we will be its slave. The flesh knows how to manipulate our emotions to demand *action*, and the flesh knows how to speak with us to make false promises as to how that action will benefit us.[94]

We cannot defeat flesh using our strength; instead, God gave us the Holy Spirit as the means to victory. The New Testament teaches that the moment someone believes, that person is born of the Spirit (John 3:5-6), regenerated by the Spirit (Titus 3:5), sealed by the Spirit (Eph. 1:13), and indwelt by the Spirit (Rom. 8:9). His life as a Christian began "by the Spirit." If that is the case, Paul asks in Gal. 3:2-3 (above),

---

94 David R. Anderson, *Bewitched: The Rise of Neo-Galatianism* (NP: Grace Theology Press, 2015), 183-185.

can he now live "by the flesh"? Paul fully expects the answer, "No way!" And here's why: "For the flesh [here our inherent ability to sin] sets its desire against the Spirit, and the Spirit against the flesh; for these are in opposition to one another, so that you may not do the things that you please" (Gal. 5:17). Plus, the flesh does not produce godly results. Rather, "the deeds of the flesh are evident, which are: immorality, impurity, sensuality, idolatry, sorcery, enmities, strife, jealousy, outbursts of anger, disputes, dissensions, factions, envying, drunkenness, carousing, and things like these" (Gal. 5:19-21).

Here's the thought: If we began by the Spirit and if the flesh produces this ugliness (sin), why would we *ever* expect to produce godly results (in this case, sexual purity) by our efforts? To be fair, not every person commits the same "deeds of the flesh" in their lives. Someone may not struggle at all with immorality, yet struggle with controlling his temper. And, by sheer willpower, someone may succeed in achieving a level of purity. We might call any purity produced by self-effort as "white-knuckle purity."[95] But, if sexual purity is a struggle (as it is for most men on some level), white knuckle, "do it yourself" purity won't bring long-term, biblical success.

Even though the flesh and the Spirit are opposed to each other, the fight isn't fair. The power of God far surpasses the power of the flesh. Check out this promise: "But I say, walk by the Spirit, and you will not carry out the desire of the flesh" (Gal. 5:16). The Greek word here translated as "walk" (*peripateō*) means "to conduct one's life, *comport oneself, behave, live* as habit of conduct."[96] Notice the promise, "will

---

95 The phrase "white knuckling" is often used in substance abuse recovery programs to describe the person who has given up drugs or alcohol without making life changes, i.e., they've given them up through will-power alone, which increases the risk of relapse (http://alcoholrehab.com/addiction-recovery/white-knuckle-sobriety/, accessed 11/30/2016).

96 William Arndt, Frederick W. Danker, and Walter Bauer, *A Greek-English Lexicon of the New Testament and Other Early Christian Literature* (Chicago: University of Chicago Press, 2000), s.v., *peripateō*. When Paul concludes this section in v. 25 ("If we live by the Spirit, let us also walk by the Spirit"), he uses a different word (*stoixeō*) translated "walk" in many translations. *Stoixeō* means "to be in line with a pers. [sic] or thing considered as standard for one's

not?" It's even more emphatic in Greek than in English: Paul uses a double negative, which is bad English but great Greek. The double negative makes it emphatic, "no way, no how, ain't gonna happen!"

Two questions pop up immediately: (1) Is this promise true? And (2) How *do* we "walk by the Spirit"? Life experience seems to contradict the statement. Every time I fail, I wonder about its validity. And when that happens, I can come to only one of three conclusions: (1) The Bible is wrong, (2) I'm misinterpreting the verse, or (3) I'm not applying it correctly. Guess which answer is the correct one? The problem here is not the truthfulness or interpretation of the verse, but the proper application of the first half of the verse. If we do not "walk by the Spirit," we cannot expect to avoid producing the deeds of the flesh consistently.

So, how *do* we walk by the Spirit? It is not that complicated! This doesn't mean it is easy to do, only that the process itself is relatively simple to describe. Galatians doesn't list "ten steps to walking by the Spirit" anywhere. In fact, the passage does not give *any* specific steps. Paul assumes his readers would understand what he meant, even as confused as they were about their initial salvation (justification) and living life as a believer (sanctification). But, that doesn't mean he gave no clues about how to walk by the Spirit:

1. We were justified by faith alone in Jesus Christ as an unconditional gift (Gal. 2:16).

2. About this justification, Paul asked, "This is the only thing I want to find out from you: did you receive the Spirit [whom we receive simultaneously with justification] by the works of the Law, or by hearing with faith?" (Gal. 3:2). The gospel was the message they heard and believed (Gal. 1:8, 11, 4:13).

---

conduct, hold to, agree with, follow, conform" (ibid., s.v. *stoixeō*). The NIV captures the idea of this word with its translation "keep in step with the Spirit." The first term speaks of lifestyle; the second gives "marching orders."

Thus, justification (being declared righteous, or "not guilty") occurs when someone *hears* the gospel message and *believes* in Jesus Christ, apart from any works. But just as justification comes by faith, so, too, does spiritual growth.

3. The believer cannot grow through self-effort: "Are you so foolish? Having begun by the Spirit, *are you now being perfected by the flesh*? " (Gal. 3:3, italics added). The implied answer is, "Of course not!" In fact, the flesh and the Spirit are opposed to each other (Gal. 5:17-18).

4. "I have been crucified with Christ [position], and it is no longer I who live, but Christ lives in me; and the life which I now live in the flesh [the physical body] I live by faith in the Son of God, who loved me and gave Himself up for me" (Gal. 2:20).

So, pulling the pieces together, sanctification (growth in general and sexual purity in particular) comes through a faith process. It starts with hearing the Word of God, and by faith believing it as true and sufficient for life. The Holy Spirit will *always* lead in accord with the Word. He might use a direct quote, a truth principle, a promise, an application of the Word, or even a "nudge," but His leading will *always* be in accord with the Word. That he does this reinforces the importance of spending time in His Word; it gives the Spirit something with which to work in our lives.

We can summarize the process of walking in the Spirit in one easy statement: *Hearing the Word with faith, then in faith responding to Him*. He will always lead us in a direction leading to our Christlikeness. We take in the Word of God and learn the truth it contains. We learn the truth that sin is no longer our legal master. We learn the truth about the indwelling Holy Spirit and the power He provides us. We believe what the Scriptures say, and we obey them as we respond in faith, trusting that the Holy Spirit leads us in the right direction through the application of the Scriptures. We believe the Holy Spirit provides us the power we need to obey as we obey.

Dave Anderson summarizes five steps that move us from slavery to freedom:

1. KNOW: *Knowing* this, that our *old self was crucified with Him*, in order that our body of sin might be done away with, so that *we would no longer be slaves to sin*; (Rom. 6:6)

2. BELIEVE: Now if we have died with Christ, we *believe that we shall also live with Him* (6:8)

3. CONSIDER (or, RECKON): Even so *consider yourselves to be dead to sin, but alive to God in Christ* Jesus. (6:11)

4. PRESENT: And *do not go on presenting the members of your body to sin* as instruments of unrighteousness; *but present yourselves to God as those alive from the dead*, and your members as instruments of righteousness to God. (6:13)

5. OBEY: Do you not know that when you present yourselves to someone as slaves for obedience, *you are slaves of the one whom you obey, either of sin resulting in death, or of obedience resulting in righteousness*? (6:16) [97]

In Romans 6, Paul wants his readers to know that the justified believer is no longer a legal slave of sin and his new identity is "crucified with Christ." The significance of this new identity impacts every dimension of life as a believer, including sexual purity. Paul says, "This is the new you. You are not a slave to sin. You have a new identity."

The key to victory is not self-effort, but dependence:

One thing God hates to hear Christians say is 'Well, I'll try.' You know why? Because that means you are going to use your own efforts to pull off what God has asked you to do. God wants to

---

97 David R Anderson and James S. Reitman, *Portraits of Righteousness: Free Grace Sanctification in Romans 5-8* (Lynchburg, VA: Liberty University Press, 2013), 72-73. The first two steps describe "hearing with faith," the last three "in faith, responding to Him."

hear you and me say, 'In dependence on your power, I *can*.' He responds, 'You're right. You can. Here's My power.' . . . This gets really practical when you start saying, 'Holy Spirit, I can't love that person in the flesh, but you can give me the ability to love him. So I am going to depend on You to give me the love I don't have in my own strength.' . . . See the difference this makes? You can take that same prayer and fill in your particular need, whether you need to control your temper, your passions, or whatever. Then when God does through you what you could never do on your own, guess what? He gets all the glory and praise![98]

Is it possible to obey without walking by the Spirit? The answer is yes *and* no. I may, on my own, delete an e-mail message with sexual content without looking at the message. But, without the attitude of faithful reliance on the Holy Spirit, we are fighting the flesh with the flesh. It's not that it's impossible to do the right things externally from time to time, but we do not bear fruit that glorifies God when we do so in our own strength (John 15:8). Long term spiritual success is impossible on our own apart from Him.

You may skip reading this note if you wish. It does not provide something necessary to know for experiencing purity. It offers brief insight "behind the scenes" tying together Galatians 2:20 and 5:16. When Paul's says, "I live by faith in the Son of God" and then "Walk by the Spirit," he does not give two different approaches to Christian living. The phrases describe the same approach, but expressed in terms of different persons in the Trinity. Jesus describes some of the interactions between the three persons of the Trinity (Father, Son, and Holy Spirit) in His final words to the disciples before His crucifixion (John 13—16):

- The *Father* would send the Holy Spirit at the request of Jesus (John14:16), in Jesus' name (14:26). The Father is

---

98 Evans, 184-185, emphasis his.

glorified both by Jesus (13:31, 17:1) and by the disciples when they bear much fruit (15:8).

- The *Son* (Jesus) said that if they (the disciples) have seen Him, they have seen the Father (John 14:7-9). He also spoke of His impending death and told the disciples it would be to their advantage that He go away (through His death, resurrection, and ascension). Otherwise, the Holy Spirit would not come to indwell them ("He will be in you," John 14:17). Jesus also told the disciples that if they abide in Him, they will bear fruit, (John 15:1-6), presumably including the fruit of the Spirit (Gal. 5:22-23) and that apart from Him [Jesus], they could do nothing (John 15:5).

- The *Holy Spirit* is called the Helper four times (John 14:16, 26, 15:26, 16:7).[99] In the first passage, He is called "another" Helper, where "another" means "another of the same kind." Thus, Jesus tells His disciples that He will send a Helper (the Holy Spirit) *like Him*. The Spirit does not speak on His own initiative (16:13) but instead testifies of Jesus (15:26), glorifies Jesus (16:14), and reminds the disciples of what Jesus said (14:6, 16:13).

Confused? To clarify, John 16:15 gives the gist of what this means: "All things that the Father has are Mine; therefore I said that He [the Holy Spirit] takes of Mine and will disclose it to you."

The Spirit would glorify the Son by expounding Him, as the Son had glorified the Father by expounding Him. The Spirit would be taking what the Father had given the Son and explaining its significance to the disciples . . . Notice that it is not the Spirit's function to attract attention to Himself or

---

99 John uses this same word (*paraklētos*) to describe Jesus in 1 John 2:1, but there it is translated "advocate" in most English translations.

> to promote Himself. As John the Baptist, His purpose is to make Jesus increase in prominence.[100]
>
> Thus, the Holy Spirit's roles are to define Christ-likeness, to mold us into His image, and to empower us to do what we need to do as an obedient son or daughter. Paul's two statements emphasize that both the Son and the Holy Spirit are intimately involved in the believer's growth, with the same goals in mind: The believer's growth into Christ-likeness as Christ lives in and through him or her.

So what does "walking by the Spirit" look like in the realm of sexual purity? Face it, guys, our sexual drive is a powerful drive. Have you ever said to yourself, "I just couldn't help it" (or some such words) when you yielded to sexual temptation? But according to the Scripture, it is *not true* that we "just can't help it." The truth is that our sexual drive is not our master. We have a choice to say yes or no; we are not obligated to our sex drive! When we grasp this truth, we are well on our way to experiencing purity This is an example of "hearing with faith"—hearing and believing what the Bible says about sin no longer being our master.

Now, imagine sitting in front of your computer. You are alone in the house, and the thought pops into your head to check out the website "woo_hoo_hoo_xxx.com." Images from past visits to the site pop into your head and your flesh starts to assert itself: "Hey, go ahead and visit the site. You'll like it! You'll feel good. And no one will catch you!" But you realize that this is your flesh speaking. You remember you are not a slave to your fleshly desires, and you recall the words "flee immorality." You choose to turn off the computer, walk out of the room, trusting God and His Word in the process. That's *hearing the Word with faith, then in faith responding to Him* in action. This illustration may seem

---

100 Tom Constable, *Tom Constable's Expository Notes on the Bible* (Galaxie Software, 2003), Jn 16:14.

simplistic, but it shows the process.[101] The more we apply the process to whatever temptation we face, the more often we'll have success. And that success comes not because of our efforts, but because of the power of God working in us, enabling us to live as He desires.

Let me close with some practical thoughts and questions to help apply the principles from this chapter.

1. If God reveals Himself through the Scriptures, what are we doing to take in Scripture?

2. Do we *really* believe we don't have to yield to sin; that sin is no longer our master? If we are honest, most would answer "no." Our experience seems to say "sin wins." Meditate on, think about, what the Scripture says and ask God to help you believe it ("Hearing with faith.")

3. If prayer is difficult, start with "bite-size" prayers. Ask God in the morning to help you be aware of Him during the day. Thank Him when He brings thoughts to your mind. "Help," and "Thanks" are legitimate prayers—they do not need to be flowery or wordy!

4. Meditate on the process of walking in the Spirit, "*Hearing the Word with faith, then in faith responding to Him.*" The better we know and practice this, the more success we will experience, and the more God will be glorified!

---

101 Handling failures is covered in Chapter Eleven.

CHAPTER SEVEN

WHAT ARE FRIENDS FOR?

Principle #2: Involve others

We met weekly. I was doing research for my Doctor of Ministry dissertation on sexual purity, and I wanted someone to ask me the hard questions. Are you looking at sites you shouldn't be? Are you acting out sexually? Are you struggling with your thought life? How is your relationship with your wife? Did you lie to me in any of your answers? I asked him similar questions. That's what friends are for.

It fascinates me that God knew every single act or thought of mine whether or not my friend asked me about them. Oddly, the fear of telling someone else about my failures or the guilt of lying to him sometimes serve as a greater deterrent than the reality that God knew all that I was doing or thinking (my sin). The good news is, God often works *in* our lives *through* other people, as he did with my friend. After David sinned with Bathsheba and worked out a scheme resulting in her husband's death, God used another person to confront him (2 Samuel 12:1-15). Nathan's three-word reply (in Hebrew), "You are the man!" boldly confronted David with the reality of his actions—actions God already knew. And that bold statement started the process of David's confession before God (Psalm 51).

Sometimes, we call this "accountability." But whatever we call it, we need others in our lives to help us grow. And those others can encourage us towards purity.

I've heard arguments against accountability: it doesn't work; we don't know how to do it well: it must cover more than just sexual purity; it is too easy to hide facts from the other person; it can turn into legalism or a "superiority complex." And all of these arguments are true—to an extent. But, occasional failures of accountability on the part of some should not force us to conclude the process cannot *ever* work.

The Bible directly says the believer is ultimately accountable to God only, specifically at the Bema seat (Rom. 14:10-12, 2 Cor. 5:10). We answer to Him, not others (at least not in an absolute sense), and we're not told to hold others "accountable." However, He *does* use interactions with others to help us grow. He did not design us to live in isolation but to live within the bigger community of "one another" (the Greek term is *allēlōn*).[102] In this book, we'll avoid the word "accountability" because of the stigma it carries in some people's thinking. Instead, we'll use the phrase "Mutual Encouragement"—ME for short—a phrase that reflects the New Testament idea of "one another."

Let's start by figuring out what ME means. It is more than a casual relationship with a friend. It's more than swapping fishing stories or talking about last night's ballgame. It's not policing another person and pointing out their failures. It's not showing 'soft' love by overlooking failures when they occur. Instead, ME is a relationship

> in which a Christian gives permission to another believer to look into his life for purposes of questioning, challenging, admonishing, advising, encouraging and otherwise providing input in ways that will help the individual live according to the Christian principles that they both hold.[103]

---

102 The word is used 100 times in the New Testament. The most common command is to "love one another" (e.g., 1 John 4:11).

103 Alan Medinger, *Journal of Biblical Counseling* 13, no. 3 (Spring 1995), 54-55, "Queries and Controversies: How can accountability be used to encourage a person in biblical change?"

Here's one "one another" passage that connects an ME friendship and sexual sin:

> Brothers, if anyone is caught in any transgression, you who are spiritual should restore him in a spirit of gentleness. Keep watch on yourself, lest you too be tempted. Bear *one another*'s burdens, and so fulfill the law of Christ. (Gal. 6:1-2, emphasis added)

Let's see how this works. Micah and Brad were close friends. Brad trusted Christ many years ago and had grown over the years in his knowledge of the Bible and in living what it teaches. He was a man of good character who demonstrated the fruit of the Spirit in his life. Micah, while having lunch one day with Brad, inadvertently disclosed he was frequenting porn on the internet. Even though Micah was a believer, he was living as a slave to sin. He chased the sexual highs he experienced while pursuing the porn, and he kept his activities under wraps.

Brad knew he had three options: he could ignore the problem (the easiest route), he could berate his friend for his sin (another easy option), or he could help his friend. He remembered being taught that "restore" was a word used in the Matthew 4:21 for mending nets, making them again useful for fishing, and that the same word was used elsewhere in Greek to describe the setting of broken bones. So Brad knew the right thing to do was help his friend deal with his sin. He knew he needed to be honest with Micah, but he needed to balance his honesty with care. He needed to avoid acting with arrogance, impatience, or anger towards Micah.

Over the next several weeks, Brad spent time with Micah. Not unexpectedly, Micah resisted Brad at first—after all, he enjoyed the feelings he experienced. Deep down, though, he knew Brad was right, and he eventually began to listen to his friend. Brad asked Micah to be honest with him about his use of the computer. In fact, he found an accountability program that would send Brad a report of *every* internet site Micah visited. And Micah knew the software was as close to foolproof as software could be. If he checked out an inappropriate site, Brad would find out about it. But Micah knew Brad's motives were solid. They talked together about why he pursued the porn. And they talked together about ways for Micah to strengthen his Christian life to identify ways for him to avoid giving in to his temptations.

But Brad knew something else he needed to do. He was aware that as a man, he could be tempted the same way as Micah. Brad wanted to make sure the time with Micah helped pull Micah up and didn't drag *him* down. So Brad called his friend Joel and asked for his help. "Joel, thanks for being my ME partner. Here's the deal: I'm working with someone who's struggling with internet porn. I can't tell you who it is, but I want to make sure I stay pure while I help him through this. Would you ask me at least once a week if I'm making healthy choices and staying away from sexual sin? The last thing I want is to give in to the very things I'm helping this guy with. Thanks!" What were the results of the process? Brad didn't slip into temptation, and Micah credits Brad's help as the key to seeing his problem and overcoming it.

This "one another" passage describes ME at its best. The way Brad helped Micah shows how this passage works in real life. Look at this passage again:

> Brothers, if anyone is caught in any transgression, you who are spiritual should restore him in a spirit of gentleness. Keep watch on yourself, lest you too be tempted. Bear one another's burdens, and so fulfill the law of Christ. (Gal. 6:1-2)

Three phrases here need clarification: (1) Transgressions (2) "Bear one another's burdens" and (3) "The law of Christ."

Transgression (paraptoma) is one of the several words the Bible uses for sin, usually referring to deliberate, specific acts of violation of God's standards. Transgressions are the specific wrongs—thoughts or actions—that we commit. It is like telling our child, "Don't put beans in your ears" and the next thing they do is put beans in their ears! That is a transgression—they violated a specific command. "To be caught in any transgression" means "to be caught committing specific acts of sin." In this case, specific *sexual* sins.

When we believed in Jesus for our salvation, God forgave us *all* our transgressions, without a single exception, whether habitual or occasional (Eph. 1:7, Col. 2:13). He forgave every sinful thought or action, no matter how small, how big, how rare, or how common. He forgave that look we gave the girl wearing the short-shorts. He forgave the repeated times we went to the internet and masturbated. He forgave when we pressured our girlfriend for sex with us before marriage. He forgave any and every sexual sin we can imagine or commit.

When we yield to temptation and commit sexual sin, we are committing the very transgressions for which Christ died. Committing these sins does not mean we are not forgiven. Instead, we are acting like disobedient children! We may experience guilt, broken relationships, or God's discipline as a loving Father (*not* as an angry judge). Plus, we miss out on God's best for our lives—freedom in Christ and glorifying God. Our sin does not change our eternal standing (the believer's security is independent of his or her behavior), but sin is always dangerous with serious consequences.

What does it mean to "bear one another's burden?" A "burden" (*baros*) is some heaviness or weight, a burden we can't carry alone. Following Hurricane Katrina, I helped a group of men repair a church in flood-ravished St. Bernard Parish. Flood waters destroyed the interior walls of the building, so to repair them, we needed to replace all the sheet rock. As anyone who has ever worked with sheet rock knows, one of the least enjoyable tasks is hauling the sheets to where they were needed. Only a fool would try to carry the sheet by himself—two four-foot by eight-foot sheets bound together weigh over 100 pounds! I decided to show my manliness by trying to lift one such bundle off the stack. What a mistake! The sheetrock was a burden (*baros*). I couldn't lift it or carry it myself. When a second person helped me with the sheetrock, though, the task was doable! The sheetrock still weighed the same, it was still awkward to carry, but the task was not impossible. That's the picture Paul paints in Galatians. We are to help each other carry their heavy burden, in this case, help each other deal with the burden of whatever sin (transgression) they are dealing with.

How does this "fulfill the law of Christ?" Of course, that requires defining the "law of Christ" correctly! When we hear the word "law," we usually think of rules and regulations. Earlier today, my wife and I went out for a cup of coffee. As we drove home, we passed a sign that said, "Speed Limit 55." That's a law—a rule about how fast we should drive. When we think of "law" in the Bible, we may think of the Old Testament law, with its 613 commands. But the "law of Christ" has nothing to do with rules and regulations. It is a different kind of law. Paul wrote Galatians to refute the ideas that justification came by following the law or that spiritual growth came by following the same law. Rules and regulations cannot give a person eternal life or spiritual maturity. What's the answer? Paul hinted at it just a few verses earlier:

> For you were called to freedom, brethren; only do not turn your freedom into an opportunity for the flesh, but through love serve one another. For the whole Law is fulfilled in one word, in the statement, "You shall love your neighbor as yourself." (Gal. 5:13-14).

Jesus directly commanded the principle in John 13:34:

> A new commandment I give to you, that you love one another, even as I have loved you, that you also love one another.

When we restore a brother caught in a trespass, we practice biblical love. Granted, most men don't think of "loving" other men as "manly." But, when we realize we are acting towards the other person the way Jesus would act towards him, we see this love is a great—and manly—response to a brother who needs help.

So now let me give you my paraphrase of Gal. 6:1-2: "If you discover a brother is involved in some sexual sin, and you are in a spiritually healthy place, and you can deal with this brother gently, do what you need to do to help him restore his life to a place of spiritual health and usefulness, helping him with the load along the way, knowing that in doing this, you love that brother the way Jesus loves each of you." This is the heart of mutual encouragement (ME). It flows from a deep, personal friendship with another believer who cares for us.

Whether we are experiencing purity or we are struggling, start developing friendships that lead to this mutual encouragement. Starting this friendship brings us to an uncomfortable point: We do not simply walk up to someone and say, "Hey Joe! Wanna hear about my sexual temptations and hold me accountable?" I suspect Joe would look at us like we were nuts! But, we do need to start the process by intentionally developing a close, solid friendship with another man or even a couple of men who understand the tug of sexual temptation. And we need men who know us well enough that we can't blow smoke past them. And *we* might be that friend for someone else! We face a couple of problems, though:

- As men, we don't have much experience talking about personal things with others, so we don't know *whom* we can trust.

- As men, we don't have much experience talking about personal things with others, so we don't know *how*!

Over the next few pages, we'll talk about some concrete steps we can take to resolve both of these problems.

How do we find that spiritually mature person who is willing to walk beside us and help? Here's a starting point: Write down the names of four men (no women!) who *might* be someone trustworthy, and with whom you might develop that ME relationship. Pray for each man, and intentionally spend time with them. Chances are, most of the names are people you spend time with anyway. Initially, just "hang out" with these guys—go to a ball game, get a cup of coffee together, go fishing. Over time, ask some probing questions like:

- How did you and your wife meet?
- When you were younger, what did you think your life would be like?
- What aspects of your Christian life come relatively easy for you?
- What do you struggle with in your life?
- What do you like about your life?
- What in your life would you like to change?

Don't try to ask all these questions in one setting—and especially not in your first meeting. These questions are only examples to help you. Add your own! What would you like to know about this other man?

Here are some ideas about what you're looking for in the answers:

- Does he seem honest with his replies?
- Is he open on some level or are his answers shallow or safe?
- Does he ask anything about you?
- If he does ask about you, does he listen to your answer?
- If you revealed something personal, how did he react?

We know no one is perfect, but we want an ME friend who has solid, godly character, something like:

> Above reproach, temperate, prudent, respectable, hospitable . . . not addicted to wine or pugnacious, but gentle, peaceable, free from the love of money . . . one who manages his own household well . . . and he must have a good reputation. (1 Tim. 3:2-7).

You might recognize these words as the qualifications for an elder, but they are not limited to elders. In other words, these characteristics serve as excellent qualities for any Christian man. The point is to look for someone who shows evidence of maturity, someone who models Christ-likeness in his life. What do others say about him? Does his life reflect what he says he believes is important? Does he keep personal information confidential?

The last question addresses the crucial issue of trustworthiness. Years ago, a friend told me about walking down a city street with a leader from his church. A scantily clad woman walked by the two of them. My friend's eyes followed the girl as she passed them, after which he asked the church leader, "Did you see that?" The leader's response: "See what?" My friend didn't believe him, shook his head, and replied, "Well, then, you're either blind or dead!" My friend realized this leader either did not understand the usual temptations men faced or, more likely, would not be honest about them.

"Generally, the safer we feel, the less our lives will be shaped and dominated by fear and shame."[104] ME requires trusting another person.

---

104 Pat Springle, *Trusting: The Issue at the Heart of Every Relationship* (Servant Publications: Ann Arbor Michigan, 1994), 18.

But trust isn't easy. In fact, *distrusting* people comes more naturally than trusting. Trust, or mistrust, comes in several forms:[105]

1. *Blind trust* trusts indiscriminately—telling anything to anyone. If we do this, we dump our lives on people who may not keep things confidential, may not care about our issues, or may even use the information against us.

2. *Misplaced trust* either trusted a person with too much too soon or trusted someone who was initially trustworthy, but later violated that trust. Misplaced trust often leads to distrust of others and an unwillingness to be vulnerable with others.

3. *Passive distrust* gives up on others. If we respond this way, we hide from others and avoid any form of conflict. We would rather stay shallow with others or physically separate from them than risk vulnerability.

4. *Aggressive distrust* controls. If we respond this way, we use our personality, talkativeness, or temper to control the other person (to some degree) and control what is said. Instead of passively avoiding others, we aggressively take control (often looking like an "out-going person") to prevent anyone from getting close to us. If *we* control the conversation, *they* cannot ask the probing questions.

None of these lead to an ME friendship. We do have another option, however:

5. *Perceptive trust* discerns the trustworthiness of others over time. As we perceptively trust others, we choose to be vulnerable and open with those who prove their trustworthiness and their genuine care for us.

---

105 All but "misplaced trust" come from *Trusting*, p. 19-21. The category of misplaced trust is my own.

Perceptive trust honestly looks at others and discerns the level of their trustworthiness. Think of this trait on a continuum:

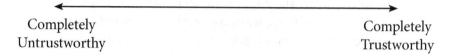

Completely   Completely
Untrustworthy   Trustworthy

Everyone we know fits someplace along the continuum. The person who violated our trust ("misplaced trust," above) would be near the far left ("completely untrustworthy"). Our best friend and spouse should be near the far right ("completely trustworthy"). Most of our friends and acquaintances fall somewhere near the middle. New relationships of necessity start further left than right since we have not yet developed any significant trust. Over time, these relationships can move towards the right as the friendship grows. Those friends near the far right are those who may be an ME friend. Of course, we do not have a real chart like this on which we rank our friends, but the concept helps us understand the idea of perceptive trust. Where a person falls on the continuum dictates the degree to which we can trust them.

How do we find the friend who may become our ME friend? By taking baby steps over time! Jesus states the principle, "He who is faithful in a very little thing is faithful also in much; and he who is unrighteous in a very little thing is unrighteous also in much" (Luke 13:10). Be warned, however! Trust requires vulnerability. We only discover the faithfulness of people when we open ourselves up and allow someone to see some part of the real us. In the process of building a friendship, we divulge "bite size pieces" about our lives. With those tidbits, the other person may reject us, violate our trust, or act trustworthy. I have friends in my life I believe I can tell anything— their trustworthiness has stood the test of time. But I also have people in my life who I thought I could trust, but later betrayed that trust and hurt me.

Developing these close friendships takes time. We cannot develop overnight the kind of relationship with another man that allows us the freedom to discuss sexual temptations, failures, and successes. In building friendships, we typically move through three broad phases:

- Forming a casual friendship, becoming an *acquaintance,* that is, someone we know and enjoy being around, but normally not someone with whom we spend much time.

- Becoming *recreational friends,* that is, friends we enjoy being with, such as a golf partner or fishing partner, but people with whom the level of openness is fairly low. Our conversations rotate around comfortable issues and rarely touch on deeply personal issues.

- Becoming a *committed friend,* that is, someone like the friend that Proverbs 18:24 describes as closer than a brother. He is the friend in whom we can confide. He is often someone who has walked through a crisis with us, and someone we know cares for us.

We will have more acquaintances than recreational friends, more recreational friends than committed friends. That is normal. The level of friendship we desire for an ME friendship is that of a committed friend.

The next obstacle, once we identify this friend who could become our ME friend, is breaking the ice and talking about sexual issues. Most men feel uncomfortable talking to other guys about sexual issues (other than locker room bragging, of course). Sexual temptation is like the proverbial elephant in the room—everyone knows it is there, but no one wants to talk about it! We can break the ice by seeing how he reacts after we bring up a "minor" sexual situation such as admitting how our eyes were attracted to the bikini-clad girl at the beach. Depending on the response, we can, over time, delve into more personal issues. How long it takes to develop the ME friendship varies from person to person. You might already have such a friend!

Asking good questions fuels a healthy ME friendship. Use the list below as a starting point. Feel free to add, subtract, or modify it to fit your situation. If you are asking the questions, make sure you ask him to dig past the simple yes or no answer when needed. Very often, "yes" or "no" by itself does not tell us much. For example, if the reply to the first question is "yes," what were the circumstances? What happened?

What have you learned about yourself? What will you do differently to prevent a slip in the future?

1. Have you been with a woman this week in a way that is inappropriate or could have looked to others that you were using poor judgment?

2. Have you been completely above reproach in all your financial dealings this week (e.g., have you spent any money on sexually explicit material)?

3. Have you viewed any explicit content this week?

4. Have you spent time regularly praying and reading the Scriptures this week?

5. Have you taken time off to be with your family this week?

6. When did you find yourself most tempted (e.g., tired, alone, after a fight with your wife, when you were discouraged, etc.)?

7. What have you learned about yourself this week? About God?

8. Have you just lied to me?

9. How can I specifically pray for you? [106]

Did you notice question eight? When we sin, we experience shame, and we are reluctant to be honest when talking about our struggles. The question doesn't guarantee that we will be honest and straightforward with our partner. It does, however, force me to think about my honesty and, if I choose to withhold the truth, I must do it twice!

---

106 Questions 1-5 and 8 are based on questions listed in Charles R. Swindoll, *Rise & Shine: A Wake-up Call* (Multnomah: Portland, OR, 1989), 211. Questions 6, 7, and 9 are mine.

The process only works to the degree that we are honest with the other person. The week I wrote this section, I heard of three people who experienced serious failures in part because they failed to be honest with their partners. One man started divorce proceedings against his wife—and no one in his accountability circle knew he was even considering such a thing. The process doesn't work perfectly, especially if we aren't honest, but it certainly provides a good start.

Accountability isn't easy, and it isn't fool-proof. But ME friends can provide a powerful tool to help us move our sins out of darkness into the light. Where light shines, darkness loses its strength. ME serves as one of the promised "ways of escape" from our temptations. Have you started looking for this friend yet? If not, don't read the next chapter until you've made a list of names of men who have the potential for serving as an accountability partner. Call one of them today, or tomorrow at the latest.

Before moving to the next chapter, let me answer five questions related to ME.

Should my wife or girlfriend be my ME partner?

I certainly do not advocate hiding our personal lives from our wives, but I do not believe this is a wise choice:

> Husbands and wives being accountable to one another is not the best arrangement. I don't believe that my wife should bear the burdens of all my struggles. Also, because of the things I need to be accountable for—my family relationships, my finances, my sexual life—are all things in which she is deeply and often emotionally involved, she cannot provide the objectivity that another man can provide.[107]

Keep in mind that when our wife or girlfriend finds out about our failure, she usually personalizes it. She asks things like, "What's wrong with me? Why am I not enough?" She compares herself to the

---

107 Medinger, 54.

make-believe of pornography, and believes she cannot measure up. Remember this from Chapter Two?

> Women feel threatened by their partner's preoccupation with pornography. These 'other' women, even though they are only pictures, intrude into the marriage relationship. It feels as though your husband is being unfaithful. Even more demeaning is the feeling that you are being compared with these women. And who can compete with airbrushed images that are touched up and unrealistic? The majority of wives can never compete with the lies portrayed in pornography.[108]

My wife knows I have an accountability partner. She told me she is glad I talk to someone, but I need my wife to be my wife, not my accountability partner. I believe another man can better understand and help deal with the issues I face.

Make your marriage stronger; grow closer to your wife.[109] But we can be—and need to be—stormproof men no matter the status of our marriage. She can pray for you, encourage you, love you, be your lover (married men!), talk with you (and you must be honest with her), tell you how she feels, care for you . . . but she should *not* be your ME friend. That kind of role should be another male who can help you with the tough issues.

I had an ME friend, but it proved to be a case of misplaced trust. Now what?

When someone we trust betrays that trust, trusting someone else becomes that much harder. I had someone hurt me recently, and it took months before I could stop filtering unrelated conversations with others through that hurt. Whether they betrayed our trust by turning on us or by revealing something confidential or by falling themselves,

---

108 Hart, Weber, and Taylor, 185.

109 See the question, "What if I am not experiencing intimacy with my wife?" in Chapter Eleven for resources with which to start this process.

the pain is real, and it impacts how we think of others. Sadly, that is the nature of close relationships. With vulnerability comes risk. But without vulnerability, our struggles stay in darkness and with rare exception, will continue to hold us in their grasp. Not everyone will fail you. In my case, several men came alongside me to encourage me and help me through the process. The benefits of an ME friendship are worth risking trust again. Start the process again with someone else.

What about seeing a counselor for help?

A counselor (whether a professional counselor or a pastor) can provide excellent help with overcoming sexual sin. In a book like this, it is impossible to cover everything that lurks in the human heart. A good counselor can help root out some of the issues that motivate our sexual sin and help discover effective solutions to those problems. Those who endured sexual abuse when children often struggle with sexual sin as adults. Those raised in harsh homes often struggle with being unable to express intimacy and openness as adults. Those who struggle with sexual addiction need help dealing with the dynamics of addiction (independent of whether the addiction is a sexual, drug, or alcohol addiction). Our ME friend may want to help, but not know how to help in these situations. A good counselor can provide substantial help. And a counselor can provide immediate help since we do not need to develop a friendship with him.

The counselor can provide great help, but he cannot replace the ME friend. Counselors help for a season; ME friendships may last a lifetime.

Shouldn't ME cover more than sexual issues?

Absolutely! Sexual purity is not the only life issue where we benefit from this kind of relationship. Since the focus of this book is purity, the focus here is (obviously) ME in the context of sexual purity. But don't limit the relationship to just sexual issues.

What is the role of the church?

The "one another" passages deal with more than sexual issues. They deal with relationships among believers, carried out within the church. God designed us to need one another, to serve one another, to love one another. We need fellowship with other believers to help keep our relationship with God fresh and vigorous. We will likely deal with sexual purity privately with our ME friend, or perhaps in a small group, rather than a larger local church setting. But we certainly need the other biblical "one another" relationships in the context of the church to help us stay spiritually healthy. When we are healthy in other areas of life, we stand a better chance of being healthy in our sexual purity. So, if you attend a church,[110] attend regularly and plug in. If you don't attend or you infrequently attend, find a church home and start attending regularly. The church should be an important part of our spiritual life.

---

110 "Church" here refers to a local body of believers, the people less so than the organization. The format of local churches varies greatly from group to group; the biblical functions of the local body are independent of form.

CHAPTER EIGHT

I THINK I CAN . . . CHANGE HOW I THINK

Principle #3: Control your thoughts

I remember one day my teenage son gave me "the look." I don't remember what triggered the "the look," but I remember it conveyed his frustration towards me at that moment. If you are the father of a teen, you know "the look" I'm talking about (I'm sure I never gave *my* dad "the look" when I was my son's age!). Being the wise father that I was (yeah, right), I gave him my look right back—the one that says "I'm your dad and you are a split second from the end of your life!" And, being the wise father that I was, I sternly told him, "You better change your attitude young man!" In hindsight, I realize how dumb was my statement to him. True, I wanted him to change his attitude, but I had not taught him *how* to change it. Changing how we think isn't easy.

Want proof? Let me try an experiment with you. Picture this in your mind: You are at a restaurant, and on the table in front of you sits one of your favorite meals. It might be a steak, chicken, seafood, Mexican food, Chinese food—it doesn't matter. In my mind, I see an 8-ounce filet mignon, cooked medium rare. Several spears of asparagus lay on top of the steak, with hollandaise sauce dripping over the side of the steak. It smells wonderful! Next to the steak is a large baked potato, covered with more butter and sour cream than a healthy man should ever eat. Cheese melts over the potato, with bacon and chives adding smell, flavor, and color to the plate. Soft dinner rolls sit in a basket to my right, and a dinner salad doused in ranch dressing sits on my left. The smells are perfect, the steam from the steak and the potato tell me everything is cooked to perfection, the colors and presentation of the meal says "I am wonderful! Eat me now!" The server just refilled my glass of iced tea. Do you have a picture in your mind? If not, stop a minute before reading on to visualize your meal. Now, picture taking that first bite. My steak is just the right color of red as I raise the first juicy, flavorful bite to my mouth.

Got the picture?

Now, STOP thinking about it. Quit it! Don't think about the meal. At all.

Are you having trouble getting the picture of the meal out of your head? I am!

Let's try it again to see what happens. This time, picture in your mind one of your favorite activities. Maybe it's replaying your best round of golf, or backpacking in the mountains, or bird hunting with a friend, or skiing some remote mountain slope. You choose. I love to fish, so I'm going to think about trout fishing near Broken Bow, Oklahoma. I have my waders on, and I'm standing in a stream, ready to cast. The stream is about 30 feet across. Steep hills form both banks. Pine trees and hardwood trees cover the hillsides. Upstream, large boulders fill the stream, and more of the same fill the stream downstream. The sound of rushing water fills my ears. The sun is low in the morning sky as its beams try to pierce through the woods to brighten the day. Sunlight dances on the water. I hear many birds, including the cry of a hawk circling overhead. In front of me, the water forms a deep pool, and occasionally I see a fish rise to the surface. I wonder if the lure on the end of my line will interest the trout at all. I cock my arm back, about to make my first cast, anticipating the fight of a rainbow trout. Everything is perfect.

Have you got your activity in mind? If not, take a few minutes to visualize it in your mind.

So, what happened to the meal you were just thinking about? (Did you think I was just going to ask you again to stop thinking about what you were doing?)

If the experiment worked with you the way it does with most people, simply telling you to stop thinking about the meal didn't make you stop thinking about it. I've had some say they succeeded, but they did so by changing what they were thinking about before we went to the second scenario. In fact, the harder we try to stop thinking about something, the more we think about it! However, when we replace what we're thinking about, the first thoughts fade away. The key to *controlling* our thoughts is *replacing* our thoughts. I wish I knew this when I told my son to "change his attitude."

The Bible teaches the process:

And do not be conformed to this world, but be transformed by the renewing of your mind, so that you may prove what the will of God is, that which is good and acceptable and perfect. (Romans 12:2)

Finally, brethren, whatever is true, whatever is honorable, whatever is right, whatever is pure, whatever is lovely, whatever is of good repute, if there is any excellence and if anything worthy of praise, dwell on these things. (Philippians 4:8)

The two key words here are *renew* and *dwell*. *Renew* means replacing the old way (being "conformed") with a new way of thinking. God's Word serves as the primary tool for renewing our mind (2 Tim. 3:16). *Dwell* means to keep our minds on the right kind of thoughts. Both work by replacing unhealthy, incorrect, unbiblical thinking with sound, correct, biblical thinking. And the process is simple—even in the realm of sexual purity.

Before you conclude that I'm nuts, and it can't be done, read the whole chapter.

First, let me remind you of the difference between *simple* and *easy*. Replacing our thoughts is a simple process, but I never claim it is easy! Simple means "not complicated." A simple process might include only a few steps, or it might be a process where each step logically flows from one to another. For example, starting a car with an automatic transmission is a simple process:

1. Put the transmission in "Park."
2. Put the key in the ignition.
3. Turn the key forward until the engine starts.
4. Let go of the key.

Assuming the car has gas and is mechanically sound, the car starts. From the perspective of the driver, the process is both simple and easy. However, a simple process may be difficult to implement. Think about weight loss: To lose weight, just burn more calories than you eat. Simple, but not easy! Losing weight requires a constant awareness of what we're eating and how we're exercising. It requires persevering until we attain our goal. It requires changing some habits, such as no donut stops on the way to the office. The process is simple: Eat less and burn more. It is simple, but for most of us, not easy. However, just because a process is not easy does not mean we cannot succeed!

The same concept applies to changing the way we think:

- Become aware of our thought(s).
- Evaluate the thought.
- Replace inappropriate thoughts.

The process is simple. Sam once told me he didn't even try to change his thoughts. He would see an attractive woman and allow his eyes to wander and his mind to follow his eyes. But after we talked about changing what we think, he realized the process was simple! As soon as he realized his thoughts were going places they shouldn't go, he started replaying his last golf game in his mind—shot by shot. Just like thoughts of fishing pushed out thoughts of the filet mignon, so too did his thoughts of golf push the sexual thoughts from his mind!

Simple, but not necessarily easy. Difficulties may arise in each step. First, I might not be critically aware of what I am thinking. Thoughts fly unchecked through my brain. I am not choosing to think about anything in particular nor am I choosing to evaluate those thoughts carefully. Not long ago, I found my mind wandering as I was "listening" to a small-group leader. I was physically and emotionally tired, so instead of paying attention to what he was saying, I let my mind wander. I became painfully aware of this when the leader asked me what I thought . . . and I had no idea what he had said. We are not always immediately aware when our thoughts wander.

That leads to my second problem. Even if I am aware of my thoughts, I am not accustomed to evaluating the quality of them. They often go unchecked.

Worse than letting them go unchecked is a faulty evaluation of them. A beautiful girl walks by and catches your eye. You soon realize your eyes are following her and your mind is going down all kinds of inappropriate paths. And your evaluation goes something like this, "She is beautiful. And I am not *doing* anything, so these thoughts are not wrong. Besides, I am a regular guy, and it is okay to think like this. I can't help it!" Do you catch the errors in this evaluation? There are at least three:

1. Jesus said if we lust for her, we have committed adultery in our heart. So, our thoughts *are* wrong, even though we do not act on them.

2. "Normal" does not define "right."

3. I *can* "help it" based on the truth of God's Word.

The third problem is, I do not know *how* to stop it. That's the goal of the rest of this chapter—how can we control our sexual thoughts?

Let me give a few typical examples of "man thought." As you read them, try to discover the problems in each:

- Bruce enjoyed watching women walking through the mall. "After all," he thought, "I'm simply enjoying the beauty of God's creation!"

- Steve loved sex. He was convinced he should enjoy sex at least once a day with his wife. He thought she should be as interested in sex as he was.

- George loved sex as well. He also thought he should be able to enjoy sex several times a week. But, he knew his wife wasn't as interested in sex as he was, so he masturbated on occasion. "I'm doing this for her. I know I want sex more than she does, so this way, I don't put pressure on her, and I don't make her feel guilty when she isn't interested."

- "Our sex life is okay, but not great. We've been married so long, the adventure isn't there, and sex is routine. Fantasizing doesn't hurt anything, and it may even help me discover some ways to add some spark!"

- "If she only took better care of herself! I wouldn't look at the pictures on the internet if she just toned up her body. Doesn't she know men are visual creatures?"

Do any of these sound like your thoughts? That's the first step. *Become aware* of our thoughts.

Second, *evaluate* the thoughts. Faulty thinking about sex plagues the mind of most men. When I first started researching these thoughts men face, I felt discouraged. Several times, I found myself saying, "Yep! That's me!" My thinking quickly moved to "Yep, That's me! What a bum—I can't change my thinking!" The first part of that evaluation might be true—that *is* me. The second part, however, is false. We can change how we think. The next few pages will help identify faulty thinking so we can change it!

1. *Incorrect views about God.* John came into my office with sadness in his eyes. "I can't ask God to forgive me *again*," he lamented. "I've confessed over and over to God about accessing internet porn. It seems I do okay for a while, but I keep slipping back into old habits. I think God must have given up on me by now." John allowed his feelings to guide his theology. True, John had other issues to work through, but he wrestled with an *incorrect view of God*. He did not fully understand the breadth of God's forgiveness. Back in Chapter Five, we talked about the person, power, and provisions of God. If I hold mistaken views about God, if I do not grasp the truth about the person, power, and provisions of God, I will easily draw incorrect conclusions about sexual sin and my relationship with God. The fact

is, God says He will forgive us whenever we confess. He gives no limits on how many times![111]

2. *Incorrect understanding of women.* Jeff, a college junior, ate dinner with our family one night. During the dinner conversation, he expressed frustration about not understanding how girls think. My wife and I had been married twenty-five years at that point, so I told Jeff that I would give him a list of everything I knew with certainty about how women thought. I handed him my business card, telling him the list was on the back. He looked at me with a puzzled look. "Ummm . . . . Mr. Fankhauser? The back of the card is blank!" I replied with a single word: "Exactly!!" He laughed, and the conversation moved on to other topics. Many men can connect with Professor Henry Higgins in My Fair Lady when he laments, "Oh why can't a woman be more like a man." Peter, however, commands us to "live with your wives in an understanding way (1 Pet. 3:7). "In an understanding way" literally means "according to *knowledge.*" Despite the fact that women and men think differently in many areas, it seems we men are, in fact, responsible for understanding them!

Here are just a few ways men and women think differently about sex:

- Most women think about sex less frequently than men.

- Most women get aroused in different ways than men.

- Most women typically think of sex within the context of a relationship; most men just think about sex!

- The way women think about sex varies with life circumstances (such as when children are in the home; where the woman is in her menstrual cycle; whether she is pre-, post- or during menopause, etc.).

- Most women rank sex lower on the list of their needs than do men.

- Most women think differently about *intimacy* than men.

---

111 This is the "family forgiveness" described in Chapter Five.

Learning to understand women takes work. But the effort is certainly worthwhile, especially for the married man learning to understand his wife.

3. *Incorrect thinking about sex being a "need."* Sex may be a powerful drive, but it is not a need. Men often think of sex as their "greatest need." This view is fraught with problems. The first is confusion between a need and a strong drive. I do not deny the male sex drive is strong and, when our wife's availability for sex does not match our drive, we get frustrated. But a subtle yet crucial difference exists between a "need" and a "drive," no matter how strong the drive. Unmet needs result in death or significant problems in life. I need food; I need water. Deprive me of either one long enough, and I will die. Love is a need and deprivation of love, especially with children, causes considerable psychological damage. However, sex is not a need. If I do not have sexual release, I will not die nor will I experience psychological harm. I might be unhappy, but I won't die!

When we define sexual desire and drive in terms of "need," we set ourselves up for problems. Think about these two faulty analyses: (1) Love is a need, and we (incorrectly!) equate sex and love. Therefore, sex is a need. (2) Sex is a need. Therefore, I must meet that need somehow. Both thoughts are wrong. Sex may be an expression of love, but, even though we often call it "making love," sex and love are not identical. We can love our spouse and be loved by our spouse without sex. I am not advocating a sexless marital relationship (the Bible surely does not promote this). Defining sex as a need influences how we handle sexual frustrations and temptations.

4. *Incorrect views about my ability to change.* I enjoy playing golf. Well, to be accurate, I *usually* enjoy playing golf! Sometimes, however, a shot goes awry, and the ball lands someplace I don't want it. I used to hate landing in the sand trap more than any other shot—even more than slashing into a water hazard. I fully believed I could not hit the ball out of the trap successfully. So, whenever I landed in the sand, I tensed up and—no surprise—hit a lousy shot. I believed the idea of me hitting the ball out of the sand was an impossibility.

This may seem like a trite illustration compared to the seriousness of sexual purity, but it illustrates the thought pattern many of us face: We believe we cannot change; we have no hope of changing; we get stuck in a pattern, whether hitting bad golf shots or practicing sin. I've heard the words too many times, "I can't stop. I can't change."

Something happened to my golf game, however. Someone took the time to show me how to hit a sand shot. And he showed me more than once. Now, when I hit my ball into the sand, I believe I can successfully hit it out. Does that mean I do it well every time? No! But, I no longer believe it is hopeless. The same goes for sexual sins. We are not hopeless. The person, power, and provisions of God *guarantee* we are not. Typically, however, our belief that we cannot change is so engrained in our thinking that overcoming it takes a lot of time and practice. For now, changing the belief that I cannot change begins by understanding that God promises the exact opposite—I *can* change (well, technically, God can change me).

5. *Allowing other women in our mind.* Let's assume someone opened up your brain and could see inside. The label on one part of your brain says, "Women I think about sexually." Are there any women in there that shouldn't be in there? These women may be a friend, someone in a picture, someone we see on the beach in a bikini, someone from the internet, or any of a thousand women who cross our paths at one time or another. The problem? These women have no place inside this part of our mind! They draw the married man away from singular devotion to the one woman who legitimately can take residence there: his wife! They occupy the space in the single man's mind reserved for his future wife.

6. *Incorrect logic.* Amazingly, my mind can convince me that just about anything is okay—even when the evidence points to a different conclusion. We call this *rationalizing*. Let's look at four forms of rationalizing: minimizing, justifying, blaming, and feeling entitled.

- *Minimizing*: I caught Ron, a high school freshman, cheating on an algebra test. He explained it away by saying it was not a big deal, that "everybody" cheats, and as long as no one was hurt, he did not do anything wrong. Sometimes we rationalize by *minimizing the seriousness of our actions*—we downplay what we do. A familiar mantra since the sexual revolution of the sixties has been "as long as no one is hurt, what two consenting people do is their business!" More recently, "If I access the internet and masturbate, I am the only affected. I didn't hurt anyone."

For the Christian man, the Bible defines the seriousness of an action. The last scenario contains at least three flaws: (1) If I am married, masturbation to a computer image means I am using a woman who is not my wife (albeit an image) for sexual gratification. (2) Whether married or single, I am not honoring the woman in the image. She, in turn, is committing sexual sin by displaying her body for men's pleasure. (3) Even if we believe masturbation is not wrong, the sexual thoughts passing through my mind during the process are wrong. *Minimizing* the actions only reflects a problem in our thinking; it does not change the seriousness of that action!

- *Justifying*: Keenan talked openly about his relationship with his girlfriend. Rob challenged him to stay sexually pure. Keenan had a short, to-the-point answer: "Why should I say no if she offers me sex? She wants it, she initiates it, so if I'm going to be her boyfriend, how can I say no?" Keenan alleges his circumstances justify his actions.

Keenan's story is not a new one. A well-known Old Testament character faced a similar situation: "**Now Joseph was handsome in form and appearance.** It came about after these events that his master's wife looked with desire at Joseph, and she said, 'Lie with me.'" Her desire was so strong; she came on to Joseph more than once. So Joseph justified sleeping with his master's wife by thinking to himself, "I am essentially a slave here. She is my master's wife, so I need to obey her. Besides, *she* initiated this, so how can I say no?"

Wait—is that how the story goes? Not even close! Here's how Joseph really responded:

> But he refused and said to his master's wife, "Behold, with me here, my master does not concern himself with anything in the house, and he has put all that he owns in my charge. There is no one greater in this house than I, and he has withheld nothing from me except you, because you are his wife. How then could I do this great evil and sin against God?" As she spoke to Joseph day after day, he did not listen to her to lie beside her *or* be with her. (Gen. 39:8-9)

When we justify our actions, we give circumstances more credit and power than they deserve. Joseph, by contrast, did not allow circumstances to dictate his actions.

- *Blaming*: "If my wife only took better care of her body! She needs to lose some weight and get in shape. Doesn't she know I'm like most guys—stimulated visually? If she took better care of her body, I wouldn't need to check out babes on the internet!" Or, "If my wife would only have sex with me more often, I wouldn't need to masturbate to relieve the sexual pressure!" Either of these sound familiar? We often blame others for our actions. This thinking takes the form "If only they would . . . then I wouldn't . . ." However, if my wife does not keep herself as attractive as I may wish or if she is not interested in sex as often as I may wish, I am still solely responsible for my actions. I cannot rightfully blame someone else, trying to make someone else responsible for my choices, attitudes, or consequences. Circumstances may make it more difficult for me, but they do not excuse my responsibility (Ezekiel 18:1-20).

- *Entitlement*: When I worked as a Human Resources manager, my administrative assistant was a life saver. I could give her a task, and I knew she would complete it on time with excellence. When she finished, she often left a one-word note on top of the completed work she left on my desk. The note simply said "Yome."

What does "Yome" mean? Pronounce it yo—me, or a little slower, you-owe-me. Instead of an IOU, she gave me a "you owe me." The "yome" note was a running joke between the two of us. But sometimes we give life a "yome." We feel entitled to sexual gratification: "I'm married, my wife owes me, but she isn't interested, I'm still entitled to sexual release. I have 'needs,' my testosterone is running full throttle, my mind is focused on sex. I deserve release!" Single guys use similar logic. They would argue, "I'm not married, I don't have the option of sex within marriage, but I'm fully male, and I'm still entitled to sexual release. I have 'needs,' my testosterone is running full throttle, my mind is focused on sex. I deserve release!"

The fundamental problem with "yome" is that it sees sex as something primarily about me. I deserve sex; I deserve a release; she needs to take care of my desires. It fails to see sex as a mutual ministry, and it fails to see self-control as a better option. It views sexual release as more important than sexual purity.

The third step in controlling our thoughts, after becoming aware of them and evaluating them, is replacing the thought. Two kinds of thoughts serve as great replacements: (1) Scripture directly, or (2) Thoughts that fit the Philippians 4:8 list: whatever is true, honorable, right, pure, lovely, of good repute, excellent, or worthy of praise. Let's think through some examples:

Situation #1: I wake up on a typical Tuesday morning. My wife left for work, and I will head to the office in a few minutes. After I've downed my first cup of coffee, I realize my mind is dwelling on sexual thoughts. I have no idea what triggered them—they are *just there*. What do I do?

Answer #1: This is a case where thinking about trout fishing or my golf game can divert my mind. My mind may snap back to the sexual thoughts, but, if it does, I need to catch another imaginary fish or play another imagery hole. I can start thinking about the day ahead of me. Or I can think of a favorite Bible passage. The key is to replace my thinking with something non-sexual and biblically sound.

Situation #2: It's the following Tuesday. I am on my way to the office, and my thoughts have wandered back to sexual thoughts. This time, I don't think about trout or golf (which I should). Instead, I start beating myself up. "This is ridiculous. I know I shouldn't be dwelling on these thoughts. I'm hopeless and helpless. I guess I can't change. It's just the way I am."

Answer #2: I realize I am involved in what some call "stinkin' thinking" about me. So, when I hear myself thinking "I can't change," I need to replace that thought with the truth, something like "I wrestle with this, but the Bible says 'sin shall not be master over you.' If the Bible says, 'Sin shall not be master over me' then my sexual thoughts shall not be master over me. And if that's true, then it means I *can* change. I am not hopeless, because of what God has done for me." Notice how understanding the foundation of our model—the person, power, and provisions of God—corrects this wrong thinking pattern.

Situation #3: I'm walking along the riverfront looking for a good cup of coffee in one of the many shops. The day is warm, and I realize some of the girls are wearing, well, not enough. One girl, in particular, catches my eyes (she doesn't know it!), and I begin to fantasize about what she looks like without the few clothes she does have on.

Answer #3: I realize I have let the wrong woman into my mind and I am certainly not honoring her with my thoughts. I need to get her out! I have several options. One is, I can pray for her. It's hard to lust after a person I am praying for! The second is, I can remind myself she is someone's daughter, and I should think of her the way I want a man to think of my daughter. So, I can think "If she were my daughter, I'd wish for her _____," filling in the blank with something good. Another is, I remind myself that she bears the image of God. Or I could remember she is (or one-day could be) someone's wife. How would I want others to think of my wife? In another version, I could change my thinking away from this girl to my family, maybe recalling a great family vacation we took together. All these options change the way I am thinking; the first three replacing the view that this girl is a sex object with a view that recognizes her as a real person and seeing her as God sees her.

Situation #4: I have been working in the living room, and my wife has already gone to bed (okay, the truth is, I was watching the Houston Astros play baseball!). I look at my wife, and think, "I'd really enjoy making love to her tonight, but she's already asleep. She's had a tough day at work, so I don't think I should wake her just for me. So, I'm going to check out www.woo_hoo_hoo_xxx. com and masturbate to relieve the tension. That way, I feel better, and I haven't disturbed her."

Answer #4: I realize I am rationalizing, minimizing my actions ("I'm doing it for her, so it's okay") and entitlement ("I deserve to release the tension"). Instead of thinking about my sleeping wife or the need to release my tension, I realize I need to do something different to occupy my mind, so I turn on the TV (back to ESPN!) or pick up a book to read. Instead of dwelling on not being able to make love to her tonight, I decided to plan a dinner date for the next evening. I decided to expect no sex as part of the evening because I don't want her to think I'm manipulating her. And if nothing "naturally" leads to sex over the next couple of days, I'll talk to her about it instead of retreating to the web. And I'll allow God's Word to change my thinking so that I can "be content in whatever state I am in."

Situation #5: I am a single man. I've been working in the living room, and now it's time for me to head to bed—alone. I wish I had a wife, and tonight I wish I had a wife because I'm thinking about sex. So, I'm going to check out www.woo_hoo_hoo_xxx.com and masturbate to relieve the tension. That way, I feel better. I can't help the fact that even though I'm single, I still have a strong sex drive."

Answer #5: I realize I am rationalizing. My thinking is laced with minimization ("I'm single with a sex drive and no other outlet. This isn't the worst choice I could make") and entitlement ("I deserve to release the tension"). Instead of focusing on my lack of a sexual partner, I realize I need to do something different to occupy my mind, so I turn on the TV (back to ESPN!) or pick up a book to read. Instead of dwelling on not being able to have sex, I decided to plan a night out the next evening, maybe a ball game. And I'll allow God's Word to change my thinking so that I can "be content in whatever state I am in."

Get the idea? We're not going to work through examples of each problem we have brought up in the book. The specific thoughts we each wrestle with are different, so my intent is to show how the process works. Hopefully, we've included enough discussion with each area of thinking that you can identify the problem and determine how to correct the problem. Before closing this chapter and moving on to the issue of wandering eyes, let me address three headaches we may encounter as we work on changing our thinking: (1) dealing with memories, (2) dealing with the "learning curve," and (3) dealing with "snap back."

When I was working on my doctoral dissertation, I learned (the hard way!) an important difference between human memory and computer memory. I made the latest set of edits on the computer before I mailed the paper to the seminary. I planned to head to bed, get up early, make any final minor changes I might need, and send it off. Sounded like a great plan—until I pulled up the computer copy to make the changes. Somehow, I saved an older copy of the paper instead of the latest copy. I lost all the edits I made the previous night! I looked hard for the newer copy, with no success. It was gone! For the average user, a deleted document disappears forever.

Too bad we cannot delete human memories as quickly and decisively—at least bad memories. I cannot delete a memory or overwrite it with a new one. Men who have been sexually active—whether with real people or pornographic images—have memories of those sexual activities. When men decide to live in sexual purity, these same memories may pop up and interfere with enjoying purity and enjoying sex with their wives. So what do we do with these memories?

I wish the answer were easy. The key is making good choices to keep from reinforcing the memories. Don't use porn anymore. Don't dwell on the old memories. Instead, replace them. The old will not go away immediately, but they will fade over time. The answer isn't easy, but it is simple. Each time the memory pops up, replace it with a different image. If you are married, replace it with a positive memory of your wife. The memory need not be sexual, just any memory or image that is pleasing and positive. If you are single, it's time to think about trout fishing or golfing again!

Keep in mind the memories will not fade overnight. The change requires time. Be persistent. Don't give up!

If changing the way we think is a new skill, being persistent means we must face a second headache: Dealing with the learning curve.

It takes time to master the process of rethinking. Just like learning to ride a bicycle, we will fall in the early phases of learning a new skill. If we've had more practice *not* controlling our thoughts (and that describes most of us!), we may find it difficult to apply the principle at first. Our enemies (the world, the flesh, and the devil) will throw darts at us telling us we are failures, which in itself is faulty thinking. It 's okay to feel frustrated as we learn the process. But just like riding a bike, if we don't give up, we'll become more proficient. Stick to the process—no matter how long it takes! Even if we only occasionally succeed, we are still doing better than when we did nothing.

The third headache I call "snap back." Why is it so easy to fall back to old thinking patterns? Let me offer two reasons: (1) Thinking inappropriately is the more natural process. Romans 12:2 admonishes us to "not be conformed to the world." The word "conformed" is in the passive voice, which means that someone or something other than me is completing the action. The world will conform me to itself unless I *actively* allow God to transform me "by the renewing of my mind." In other words, it takes no work or effort on my part to think like the world thinks! (2) I have practiced thinking inappropriately for a long time. An old (and incorrect) proverb says, "Practice makes perfect." The more accurate version goes something like this: "Practice perfects that which you practice." In other words, when we practice the wrong thing, we perfect the wrong thing! Want proof? Just look at my golf swing. When we have perfected something, we will snap back to that practiced position if we do not make deliberate choices to do differently. We find ourselves snapping back when we are tired, when we let our walk with God slide, or when we stop practicing the new skill. Don't let "snap-back" deter you from moving forward. Keep practicing—practicing the right thing, of course!

We can change our thinking. We can control our thoughts. The process is simple, but not easy. It takes time; it certainly takes diligence. But I know I can change my thinking. How do I know? The Word of God tells me I can be transformed. It tells me to think of biblical passages or of those things that are good. It says I should set my mind on "things above." And the Holy Spirit gives me the power to do so.

CHAPTER NINE

WHAT YOU SEE IS NOT WHAT YOU GET!

Principle #4: Control your eyes

The mailboxes for the apartment complex stood next to the pool area. And sure enough, when I went there one day to get the mail, a woman wearing a skimpy bikini stood up by the pool. Do you know how hard it is to put the key in the mailbox lock when you lock your eyes elsewhere? I quickly turned back towards the mailbox, got my mail, and left. The entire distraction took only a few seconds, but it reminded me how easily our eyes wander and get us into trouble! The bikini-clad woman did nothing wrong; the problem was controlling my eyes!

Here are three truths about men and their eyes:

1. Most, if not all, men are visually stimulated.

2. Most men enjoy the female form.

3. Men's eyes almost have a mind of their own and lock on to the female form with no real effort on our part!

God designed this attraction to women as a good thing. Remember Adam's response upon waking from "surgery" and seeing the woman for the first time? To say he was excited and pleased is an understatement! But ever since the fall, the eyes cause us trouble. The design of the opposite sex is not the problem, nor is the eye itself or even enjoying what we see. The problem comes when our flesh interprets what we see and then guides the next step. My survey asked men if they were aware of their eyes lingering inappropriately. Only 25% of the respondants replied "rarely" or "never." That means the other 75% either *cannot* control their eyes or at times *will not* control their eyes. We need to add to the three truths above a fourth truth about our eyes:

4.   We *can* control where we look.

Job did. He said, "I have made a covenant with my eyes; How then could I gaze at a virgin?" (Job 31:1). Solomon admonished his son with these words:

> My son, give attention to my words; Incline your ear to my sayings. Do not let them depart from your sight; Keep them in the midst of your heart. For they are life to those who find them and health to all their body. Watch over your heart with all diligence, For from it flow the springs of life. Put away from you a deceitful mouth and put devious speech far from you. *Let your eyes look directly ahead* And let your gaze be fixed straight in front of you. Watch the path of your feet And all your ways will be established. Do not turn to the right nor to the left; Turn your foot from evil. (Proverbs 4:20-27, emphasis added)

Jesus taught that to control the eye was crucial:

> If your right eye makes you stumble, tear it out and throw it from you; for it is better for you to lose one of the parts of your body, than for your whole body to be thrown into hell. (Matthew 5:29, see also 18:9)

He later says this about our eyes:

> The eye is the lamp of the body; so then if your eye is clear, your whole body will be full of light. But if your eye is bad, your whole

body will be full of darkness. If then the light that is in you is darkness, how great is the darkness! (Matt. 6:22-23)

Adam and Eve fell in part because the tree was "a delight to the eyes."

The lack of control of our eyes comes with a high price. David's lack of eye control failed him. The story of his failure is all too familiar:

> Then it happened in the spring, at the time when kings go out to battle, that David sent Joab and his servants with him and all Israel, and they destroyed the sons of Ammon and besieged Rabbah. But David stayed at Jerusalem. Now when evening came David arose from his bed and walked around on the roof of the king's house, and from the roof *he saw a woman bathing*; and the woman was very beautiful in appearance. So David sent and inquired about the woman. And one said, 'Is this not Bathsheba, the daughter of Eliam, the wife of Uriah the Hittite?' *David sent messengers and took her*, and when she came to him, he lay with her; and when she had purified herself from her uncleanness, she returned to her house. The woman conceived; and she sent and told David, and said, 'I am pregnant.' 2 Samuel 11:1-5 (emphasis added)

Whether David should have gone to battle or not is not the key problem. Neither is Bathsheba's bathing on the roof. The problem lies in the two words "saw" and "sent." His eyes saw the woman, and he was "carried away and enticed by his lust." This eye problem led to further sexual sin, a "crisis pregnancy," the murder of the woman's husband, Uriah, and a host of trials in David's life and reign. David's own words describe the anguish he experienced because of his sin, "When I kept silent about my sin, my body wasted away through my groaning all day long. For day and night Your hand was heavy upon me; My vitality was drained away as with the fever heat of summer" (Psalm 32:3-4). Imagine with me a different story. What if the story went like this:

> Now when evening came David arose from his bed and walked around on the roof of the king's house, and from the roof he saw a woman bathing; and the woman was very beautiful in

appearance. And he remembered from the Law, the Law he loved, that Potiphar's wife wanted Joseph to sleep with her. He remembered Joseph's words "How then could I do this great evil and sin against God?" and that Joseph did not listen to her to lie beside her. Joseph left his garment in her hand and fled. David remembered and said to himself, "How then could I do this great evil and sin against God?" He turned his eyes away and went back into his house.

Sadly, this story is fiction, because David "saw and sent" instead of "saw and turned away." *David didn't, but we can see and turn away!*

Here is the million-dollar question: Will God ever ask us to do something He does not equip us to do? In other words, will God hold us accountable for something He knows we cannot possibly do? The question answers itself: God *does* expect us to control our eyes and therefore He *does* give us the provisions to do so! The key which unlocks the ability to control our eyes is the power of the Holy Spirit (Gal. 3:3b-5). Our flesh cannot control our flesh. We can fake it for a while, but ongoing success comes when we rely on God's power and provisions.

That leads us to another simple, but not necessarily easy, solution. Controlling my eyes requires only four steps, all done in dependence on the Spirit to empower us:

- Choose to protect our eyes.
- Address thoughts that arise when we respond to what we see (Chapter Eight).
- Remove the "eye candy" (sexual images) when we can.
- Look someplace else when we cannot!

I can hear a thousand objections to this simple solution, not least of which is "You must be kidding. I've tried over and over, but my eyes seem to have a mind of their own! No matter how hard I try to control them, they wander where they want." But again I'll say they do not have to wander! Job's eyes didn't wander. He made the decision to protect his eyes. He said he made a covenant with his eyes so he would not "gaze at a virgin." We do not know any of the details of this covenant; we have only this one line in Scripture that mentions it at all. But if we take his confession at face value, he succeeded. How about if we begin the process by making a similar covenant with our eyes? At the end of this chapter, I've included a covenant we can sign. Will you sign it? *Choosing* to protect our eyes is the first step to controlling our eyes.

Remember the difference between outside (objective) and inside (subjective) temptations? It's not what we see that turns that sight into "inside" temptation; it's what we *think* about it. Some sights are overtly sexual (nudity, for example). Some are not (the woman wearing blue jeans, for example). But if my thoughts start focusing on the *body* of the woman in those jeans, I've started moving the wrong direction. Eye problems actually cannot exist in isolation. If I *think* properly about what I see, the eye problem goes away.

Let's assume we chose to protect our eyes, and we deal with the whatever thoughts arise. The next two steps are simple: Remove the source when we can and look away when we cannot!

What sources feed "eye candy" to our eyes? The list below is likely incomplete (add anything that comes to your mind that is missing), and not listed in any particular order. True, some examples seem more innocent than others—more on that later.

- *Media (movies, television, print, pornography).* Some movies are highly sexual (so-called "adult movies"). Some are "mainstream" that contain sexual content (theatrical releases, movies produced by premium movie channels like HBO, etc.). Television includes premium movie channels, but also advertisements or shows with strong sexual messages (I can think of several such shows that affirm casual sex and portray hopping from bed-to-bed as "comedy"). Pornography is the most sexually-explicit form of media. We may access porn intentionally, but sometimes it shows up unintentionally.

- *Advertising.* While public advertising in the United States places some restraints on sexual content, many ads still use sex as a marketing ploy. For some products (such as that famous lingerie company), such advertising makes sense (even though it is problematic from a purity standpoint); for some, it does not. Under the mantra "sex sells," sex appeal rarely has much to do with the product. An advertisement for a certain perfume uses a strongly suggestive scenario for the entire commercial. The perfume itself only shows up for a few seconds at the end.

- *Women in public.* Some dress provocatively. I recently attended a wedding where one guest wore a dress that was too tight, too short, and cut too low. Although I cannot say with certainty, it seems impossible to me that she did not know how she looked in that dress. Others simply dress sexily. The clothes show some skin and accentuate the body but are not overtly provocative. And some just wear "regular" clothes that are not sexy in themselves, but still attract our attention (a beautiful dress, blue jeans, etc.).

Women wearing swimsuits attract our eyes. The bikini caused controversy when it first appeared in 1947. It was not the first two-piece swimsuit, but this one started the rage for two-piece suits. Today, scanty two-piece suits are considered normal in our culture and much of the world. Some leave very little to the imagination.

- *Nudity in public.* See-through clothes. Strip joints. "Clothing optional" beaches. And sometimes, nudity in unexpected places! A few years ago, my wife and I visited a resort in Hot Springs, Arkansas with two other couples. We lounged in the hot tub outside for a while, then my wife and I left the tub while the other couples stayed a bit longer. Later, one of the guys told me a man and a woman came to the tub. The woman wore a robe, but when she took it off to enter the tub, she had nothing on underneath. Unexpected, to be sure!

Get the idea? "Eye candy" permeates our world.

What about the "more innocent" examples? The bestseller *Don't Sweat the Small Stuff... And It's All Small Stuff*[12] was published nearly twenty years ago. In many life situations, the title fits. However, in the realm of sexual purity, the "small stuff" makes a difference. I could watch the sitcom "Two and a Half Men" and never act out sexually as a result. However, the actions and words of the lead character plant seeds of a non-biblical philosophy in our brain. They move us in the direction of conforming to the world, rather than being transformed. Rather than feed our minds with sexual content (albeit mild) from these "more innocent" examples, wisdom would say be careful with what we take in. Of course, I am not saying this "small stuff" is necessarily wrong (as I could about porn). I'm just urging us to be careful. Sometimes little things fuel the fire and make it just that much harder to make good choices when stronger temptations come along.

Now that we have an idea of the sources of "eye candy," we need to deal with them. The two simple steps are, remove the source when we can and look away when we cannot!

Most sources are out of our direct control, but some we can control. How can I remove those sources? Here are a few examples. Each of us must look at our world to decide what we need to do:

- Do the premium movie channels cause you problems? Cancel them!

- Do you ever use pay-per-view to watch porn? Ask someone in your home (or a friend if you live alone) to set parental controls on your TV with a password of their choice on your TV so that that you cannot order any inappropriate movies, If you are in a motel by yourself, ask the desk clerk to block pay-per-view.

- Avoid going to the pool or beach by yourself.

---

112 Richard Carlson, *Don't Sweat the Small Stuff... and It's All Small Stuff: Simple Ways to Keep the Little Things from Taking Over Your Life* (New York, NY: Hyperion, 1997).

- Throw away swimsuit issues or lingerie catalogs that come in the mail *before* looking at them.

- Change your driving route if you pass strip joints (if they are a temptation for you) or other sexual images. Years ago, the milk industry used the slogan, "Milks Does a Body Good." On one road I drove regularly, a billboard posted that slogan with the picture of a girl in a skimpy bikini. I needed to—and did—change my driving practices to avoid that sign.

- Change the channel or turn off the TV when something sexual pops up, whether a commercial, program, or movie.

- Protect your electronic devices to make it harder to access inappropriate sites.

- If you own porn, destroy it. Don't just throw it away—it's always possible to pull it out of the trash any time. Delete files on your computer, then empty the trash. Melt CDs over a fire.

That list should help you get started. What do *you* need to do in your world?

Remove the sources that you can. But most of us will need the second step—look elsewhere—more than the first.

The simple solution when faced with unexpected and unwanted images, whether live, in print, or on a screen, is to look elsewhere. Stephen Arterburn calls it bouncing the eyes, Joe Dallas calls it diverting, but whatever you call it, the concept is the same: The *instant* we are aware our eyes are looking where they shouldn't be, look at something else! No matter how strong the visual attraction, the temptation to look, linger, or leer is *not* more than we can endure. The Bible promises that with every temptation, we have a "way of escape," *even for our eyes.*

The process certainly *feels* hard to do. Part of the reason for the difficulty is that we did not learn the right way early in life, so we have practiced the wrong way for years!

Since we are visual creatures, our eyes do not know the difference between appropriate attraction and inappropriate looking, lingering, or leering. The eyes only identify the attractions. The brain must process what we do next. God designed man's attraction to the female form as a good thing. Noticing an attractive woman is not, in itself, a problem. Being attracted to our wife is a good thing (Prov. 5:19, Song of Solomon 4:1-7). The problem comes when our sinfulness directs our eyes or redefines what we see.

Let's say we are sitting in a coffee shop on a warm afternoon. In walks a beautiful young woman, wearing short-shorts and a bikini top. The first glance—noticing that she is attractive—is not a problem. But our brain processes the vision and decides we need to watch her, at least (in theory) subtly! We check out her body, up and down. We peek down her top, hoping to see just a bit more if she bends over. We repetitively look over at her, hoping she doesn't notice. She probably does notice, by the way, and we certainly are not honoring her when we use her body for our visual pleasure. Does the scenario sound like something you'd do?

The simple—but not easy—solution is, look somewhere else! Look out the window. Look across at another part of the shop. Look at your table. Look at your tennis shoes. Just look someplace else. That's the idea. No matter what attracts our eyes, look someplace else. Anyplace else.

Joe Dallas recommends another helpful step when we turn our eyes elsewhere:

> Then you *breathe*, deeply and quietly. The value of deep breathing is that, in tough situations, it helps you regain control. If you're very angry and ready to pop someone, for example, a few deep breaths can calm you down. Or when you're panicking, it's amazing what deep breathing does to stabilize you. Or, in this case, to cool you down and prevent stimulation from going any further.[113]

---

113 Joe Dallas, *The Game Plan* (Nashville, TN: W Publishing Group, 2005), 141-142.

When the "eye candy" appears, take a deep breath and look away. Train yourself. You can do it. To what do we turn our gaze? Towards anything or anyplace safe! I have admired the top of my tennis shoes many times when I am walking with someone, and my radar eyes alerted me to an attractive person nearby.

We may conclude it's hard, if not impossible, to control our eyes. We have so much practice letting our eyes roam where they will (after all, it's "natural" for a man!), that training them to act differently is difficult. Unlearning and relearning is a complicated process. Chances are before we made a choice to control our eyes, we were not aware of how many ways our eyes wandered and where they lingered. Our eyes, practiced in searching for the female form, say "Cute girl coming our way!" Our brain responds, "Okay—enjoy!" and, after a few minutes, our brain kicks in again and says, "Yikes! Wrong answer! Look away!" We reflect on the adventure and conclude "I blew it—again." Sound familiar?

Make the choice to persevere in unlearning and relearning. When I took golf lessons, the first few days applying what I learned were awkward. My shots did not improve—in fact, I was so aware of the struggle, I wanted to go back to my old swing (which, by the way, would be a terrific approach if the goal were slicing the ball deep into the woods). And, for several rounds after those lessons, I had to think about every stroke: Put your feet here; hold the club like this; turn, don't rock; keep your head down. I wondered if it was worth it. The old way certainly did not yield decent scores, but at least I did not feel like a complete klutz in the tee box. But my score did not improve—at least not right away.

Something happened, however. The more I practiced, the more "normal" the new swing felt and the less I had to think about every step. The more I practiced, the better the results of my new swing. And my game improved. Had I given up during the time between when I learned my new stroke and when I became reasonably competent with it, my game would have fallen back into the doldrums. But practicing the right things trains us to do the right things, whether golf or controlling our eyes. Press on. The long term results outweigh the short term pain. Keep doing the right things, relying on the Holy Spirit as you move forward, and as you do so, the process will become easier. The Spirit changes us, and we fail less often.

How long does it take to change? Stephen Arterburn says practicing something for six weeks will change what we practice into a habit.[114] But whether it takes days, weeks, or even months, the new habit allows us to glorify God with our eyes for a lifetime. We *can* stop presenting the members of our body—our eyes—to sin as instruments of unrighteousness. We *can* present ourselves to God as those alive from the dead, and our members—our eyes—as instruments of righteousness to God (Rom. 6:12-13). Listen to this true story of using the eyes this way:

A couple of years ago a friend of mine gave me tickets to a Dallas Mavericks basketball game on the floor. Center court. You know—those $4,000 seats no real people can afford? I took my son who at the time was about nine or ten years old. We were sitting there with our feet right on the court. During the first timeout, as is normal at a Mavericks game, we heard over the loudspeaker system, "Ladies and gentlemen, welcome the best dance team in the NBA, the Dallas Mavericks Dancers!" Now, when you are on the front row, those girls are *really* close. They come strutting out. We're right there, they are doing their dance, and my son's eyes are big as saucers! He leaned over to me and said, "Daddy? Those girls don't have enough clothes on, do they?" I said, "They don't have *near* enough clothes on! I tell you what, buddy, you look at me," and I grabbed his little chin (his eyes came with the chin). "Look at me, look at me," I said, "How about we look at each other every time these girls come out. Let's talk, all right?" So there we were, and every time the dancers came out in front of us, we stared at each other. About halfway through the game, I said to my son, "You know what? We can choose to allow our eyes to be used as instruments of wickedness and we could watch those girls. We would be doing them a disservice, we would be doing ourselves a disservice,

114 Arterburn and Stoeker, p. 145-146.

I would be doing my wife a disservice and you your future wife, too. A lot of problems there. We can just look at each other, or we can choose to use our eyes as instruments of righteousness. How could we do that during this time?" We had a little conversation about it. I said, "I've got an idea. Let's look at all the men who are watching the girls." So I turned around, he looked with me, and we looked up in the stands. And here is what grieved me as I looked at these guys: Their wives sitting next to them, and I know they were thinking, "He hasn't looked at *me* like that in years." And my heart grieved for these marriages all around the place. Thousands of them. I said, "Son, how about we just choose a couple each time the girls come out and we pray for that couple?" So now, every time we go to the Mavericks game, when the girls come out, we turn and look for a couple where the guy is focused on the girls and the wife looks like she is struggling. We pray for them during the whole time out. And God uses our eyes as instruments of righteousness instead of instruments of wickedness. It's done in the power of the Spirit; it's not done in the flesh but brothers, here's the good news. *It can be done!*[115]

We *can* do it. God empowers us to do so; He says we can do so.

---

115 Pete Briscoe, Senior Pastor, Bent Tree Bible Fellowship. He told this story during a presentation at the Pine Cove Christian Camp Men's Retreat, February 2006. Used with permission.

"I have made a covenant with my eyes; how then could I gaze at a virgin?" (Job 31:1)

A Covenant for Our Eyes:

Recognizing that men (including me) are stimulated sexually by what we see;

Recognizing it is far too easy in our world to find visual stimulation, even without trying;

Recognizing women are created in the image of God; and

Recognizing every woman is someone's daughter, and perhaps someone's wife or sister,

I make this covenant before God with my eyes to treat other women honorably with my glances, to avoid looking where I should not look (whether towards a woman in person, in print, or on the screen) and direct my eyes toward that which is good.

I desire to walk in purity, making godly choices by avoiding all inappropriate sources of visual sexual gratification and by seeking to glorify God and to honor women with my eyes.

I desire that He change me from the inside out. I know I cannot do this successfully and regularly in my own power, so I desire to hear the Word with faith, then in faith respond to Him.

When I am aware I failed, I will confess my failure before God, knowing He forgives.

When I recognize success, I will give Him the praise.

_____   _____

Signed   Date

_____   _____

Witness   Date

CHAPTER TEN

RUN AWAY!

Principle #5: Flee!

We were fishing on Coleto Creek Reservoir on a warm summer night. We tied the boat to an old tree standing in the lake, hoping to find crappie lurking near that tree. To improve our chances, we put out a floating light that shined into the water. Much like an outdoor light attracts bugs, the floating light attracts bait. The bait fish attract larger fish—our quarry! We dropped our baited hooks under the light as well, hoping the fish would take our bait.

The bait did not realize it, but by swimming *toward* the light, they were swimming towards harm's way. I doubt they thought, "Cool! I'll swim toward the light so I can become dinner for a bigger fish!" Instead, they should think, "This is dangerous. Swim away!"

In whatever way it presents itself, sex acts as that light for most men. We are drawn to it. But, just like the small bait fish drawn to the light, apart from sex within marriage, we need to "swim away." The Bible uses the phrases "flee from" and "abstain from" sexual immorality:

For this is the will of God, your sanctification; that is, that you *abstain from sexual immorality*; (1 Thessalonians 4:3)

Now *flee from youthful lusts* and pursue righteousness, faith, love, and peace, with those who call on the Lord from a pure heart. (2 Timothy 2:22)

Flee immorality. Every other sin that a man commits is outside the body, but the immoral man sins against his own body. (1 Corinthians 6:18)

The concept is simple: When immorality rears its head, turn and run!

If we practice the skills already discussed in this book, we have fewer reasons to flee because we're already dealing appropriately with many sexual situations. But sometimes, no matter what we're doing to protect ourselves, we encounter situations from which we must flee (just ask Joseph!). And sometimes, we'll "wake up" mid-situation (a situation of our own doing), realizing we need to flee. We'll look at four typical categories of these situations: (1) Sexual distractions, (2) Use of electronic devices, (3) Sexual immorality through the commercial sex industry, and (4) Sex with others.

Sexual distractions

Sometimes, sexual distractions just pop up. I was at the mall shopping for a Christmas present for my wife. I wasn't really sure what to get, so I roamed from store to store, looking for ideas. I rounded one corner only to find that famous lingerie store, with bigger-than-life posters of sexy models wearing skimpy lingerie. On another occasion, I was at a beach during warm weather. No surprise, I saw at the same beach several women wearing swimsuits, some quite skimpy. On the one hand, I did nothing overtly sexual as a result of either the posters or the women on the beach. But on the other hand, each caught my eye, engaged my mind, and appealed to my fleshly desires. What can we do with these distractions?

Avoid when possible those places we know about that present sexual distractions to us (like the lingerie store). For example, unless I need that one area of the mall, I should not go near the lingerie store. But if you cannot avoid it, or it pops up uninvited, use the skills discussed in Chapters Eight and Nine to control your eyes and change your thoughts. Take a deep breath and look elsewhere. Remember the covenant you made like Job's, "I have made a covenant with my eyes; how then could I gaze at a virgin [this woman or poster]?" (Job 31:1).

The more dangerous sexual distraction is "the other woman."

I once watched a herd of elk in the Cascade Mountains. Each herd has one dominant bull (male) and many cows (females). Other bulls express interest in the cows, but the dominant bull fights them off for his own. Every bull elk has eyes for more than one female—each would like the entire herd under his control. I saw another animal in the same mountains: a bald eagle. Bald eagles are monogamous and mate for life. Only if a mate dies does a bald eagle choose another mate. Regardless of how many eagles live in a region, the male and female have eyes only for one another.

God created us like eagles, yet in our fallen state, we act like elk. God designed each of us to be a one-woman man (1 Tim. 3:2). He designed us to have eyes only for one, yet we sometimes look at the entire herd and want more, and sometimes they come after *us*. Whether we chase them or they chase us, elk mentality runs counter to our eagle design. What do we do with women other than "the one?" The problem has plagued us for ages. Listen again to the voice of the Proverbs:

My son, give attention to my wisdom ... for the lips of an adulteress drip honey and smoother than oil is her speech; but in the end she is bitter as wormwood, sharp as a two-edged sword. Her feet go down to death, her steps take hold of Sheol. She does not ponder the path of life; her ways are unstable, she does not know it. Now then, my sons, listen to me and do not depart from the words of my mouth. Keep your way far from her and do not go near the door of her house, or you will give your vigor to others and your years to the cruel one; and strangers will be filled with your strength and your hard-earned goods will go to the house of an alien; and you groan at your final end, when your flesh and your body are consumed; and you say, 'How I have hated instruction! And my heart spurned reproof! I have not listened to the voice of my teachers, nor inclined my ear to my instructors! I was almost in utter ruin in the midst of the assembly and congregation.' Drink water from your own cistern and fresh water from your own well. Should your springs be dispersed abroad, streams of water in the streets? Let them be yours alone and not for strangers with you. Let your fountain be blessed, And rejoice in the wife of your youth. As a loving hind and a graceful doe, let her breasts satisfy you at all times; be exhilarated always with her love. For why should you, my son, be exhilarated with an adulteress and embrace the bosom of a foreigner? Proverbs 5:1-20

Get the picture? Other women look good, but the result is anything but good. The married man's pleasure should be with his wife. Of course, legitimate friendships with the opposite sex are fine. That is not the issue here. The "other woman" becomes an issue when she distracts us sexually. Relationships with the "other woman" take three forms, all dangerous: (1) a fantasy relationship, (2) a flirtatious relationship, and (3) a physical relationship.

In the fantasy relationship, we imagine something going on with the other woman. Internally, we begin to long for them. We may or may not act on the fantasy, but we are no longer monogamous in our thinking!

The flirtatious relationship goes further. We flirt using sexual innuendo. We allow the conversation to go down—or we take it down—troublesome paths. We might talk about personal things which are too personal to talk about outside of marriage. So, thoughts like "she understands me better than my wife" or "she is sure attractive—I am interested!" pop up. Emotional bonds develop. Such emotional connections beyond friendship may lead to physical connections. If married, these emotional connections violate the husband and wife "one flesh" relationship designed for us by God.

And physical relationships go further yet. Tom and Linda were married—but not to each other. Each left his or her partner, and the two moved in together. "Our prayer life is better than it has ever been. We enjoy being with one another." They violated relational boundaries, which eventually lead to their sexual union. Because they poured into each other emotionally and spiritually instead of into their spouses, they rationalized that their new relationship with each other was okay before God! In this case, Tom allowed the "other woman" to invade his wife's bed. Two marriages destroyed by one man going too far with "the other woman."

So far, we have talked about relationships where the man allows the other woman access to his heart. But we must also protect ourselves from the woman who hunts the man. Too many times I hear of pastors succumbing to "the other woman," sometimes instigated by the woman. Perhaps the woman developed an unhealthy emotional connection when the pastor helped her work through some crisis in her life; maybe instead she wanted to bring down someone in power. A pastor I know told me of one such woman who came into his office under the auspices of a "counseling need." It is possible she was not on the prowl, but every instinct he had said otherwise. He had two choices: flee or don't flee! He chose to flee—he canceled the appointment and referred her to an outside counselor.

So what do we do with "the other woman"? Look again at Proverbs 5, "Keep your way far from her and do not go near the door of her house. And (if married) rejoice in the wife of your youth." Sounds a lot like "Flee! Run away!" Remember Joseph and Potiphar's wife? He fled. We need to emulate Joseph's character and flee as well!

If we discover even a hint of being attracted to another woman, do whatever is necessary to avoid one-on-one time with her. Replace/change the way you think about her (Chapter Eight) with thoughts of Scripture, or of the woman's real identity (someone's daughter, wife), or of some other positive thought. Do this as often as necessary to drop her down a level in your thinking below "sexual distraction." Do not succumb to the lie, "I can't stop thinking about her. Maybe there's something here I should pursue."

If you must interact with her (and I mean a "real" must, like a business meeting, not a justifying "must"), do so in a public place. If privacy is necessary, do so in a room with a window so that people could observe you if they so choose. And if such a meeting is unavoidable, tell your ME friend about the meeting so he can ask later about your behavior.

When you are with her, do as Stephen Arterburn recommends: "Play the dweeb."[116] Talk "guy stuff" in which she has little interest!

---

116 Arterburn, 170-171.

Typical topics—but certainly not universal—include football, baseball, hunting, fishing, or *any* subject that bores her! If you are married, talk about our wife and family *ad nauseam* to communicate your love for and commitment to your family. It does not matter if she thinks you are a "dweeb." In fact, that's the goal! Our goals are our purity and her honor.

The key to dealing with sexual distractions is to act quickly and decisively. Flee!

Electronic devices

The internet caused an explosion of growth for the porn industry. Magazines, videos, and DVD's have long been available, but the internet allowed people to bring porn into their home immediately, sometimes at no cost, without the "discomfort" of buying it in a store or receiving it in the mail. Many electronic devices (computers, tablets, phones) allow internet access and thus can serve as mediums for pornography. The problem is not the device itself; the problem is how we use it. Not only can many devices access the internet, but the vast availability of free Wi-Fi and the small size of tablets and phones make for easy access anytime and anyplace with little risk of being caught. The suggestions that follow cannot guarantee we will avoid inappropriate sites but implementing them will improve our odds! Ultimately the "want to" factor combined with walking in the Spirit (Hearing the Word with faith, then in faith responding to Him) give the keys to our success:

- Install accountability software that reports your computer activity to an accountability partner (your ME friend). My package of choice for all devices as of this writing is CovenantEyes™ (www.covenanteyes.com). Check reviews of various packages based on your devices before selecting an option.[117]

---

117 Search for reviews using a phrase like "internet accountability for Christians" and read reviews or comparisons of the services offered before making your choice. Two such sites are https://www.thoughtco.com/top-

- Install a filter to block some content from your device. Get someone else to set the password to prevent you from disabling the filter, do not let them share it with you.

- Avoid accessing the internet when your risk of falling to temptation is high, such as late at night, when you feel lonely, when you are discouraged, etc. (Chapter Three).

- When the temptation to access inappropriate material strikes, turn off your device. Put it down. Walk away from it. Avoid using it again until you have dealt with the temptation.

- If you have children under 18 years old in your home, set up parental controls on any device they may use. Be counter-cultural—do not let a minor under your control have unprotected access to electronic devices. The risk is too high!

Electronic devices are dangerous, but the danger is manageable. Fleeing immorality on them requires us to do all we can to prevent accessing sexual sites. Flee!

Sexual immorality through the commercial sex industry

"The sex industry consists of any business whose earnings derive from the exchange of money for sexual favors or the representation of sex in print, photographic media, video, or the Internet."[118] This section briefly addresses those businesses who derive their earnings from sexual favors, specifically, prostitution, strip clubs, and "adult" stores. The solution to the stores and clubs is simple: (1) Never step foot inside one, and (2) Should you enter, leave immediately. These businesses attract people by providing easy access to sex and sexual products while serving no useful services. They simply promote sexual sin. Call your ME friend when temptation tugs you to go in; seek help from a pastor or counselor if this is a frequent problem. Something

---

christian-internet-filtering-services-701270 and http://www.safefamilies. org/SoftwareTools.php, each accessed July 7, 2017.

118 http://medical-dictionary.thefreedictionary.com/sex+industry, accessed July 4, 2017.

is driving you; they can help you discover what that may be. Don't go in!

Prostitutes offer sex with another person but with no intimacy, other than purely physical, and no real relationship whatsoever. They substitute real intimacy as God designed it with paid-for sex. And some of these prostitutes allow unhealthy sexual deviancy. Prostitution is legal in certain countries and within a few counties in Nevada (under certain conditions), but "legal" does not make it "right." Proverbs makes it clear we should avoid sex with "the adulteress" (such as a prostitute) and "keep away from her, not even to go near the door of her house" (see Prov. 5:1-20). Sex with a prostitute or a "hook up" is the most impersonal sex a person can have with another person.

If you engage in this kind of sex, talk with a pastor or counselor to help uncover why such activity appeals to you. Indulging in this sort of sin may result in harsh temporal consequences (such as the possibility of disease or arrest, damaging or destroying your marriage or dating relationship). Seeking such impersonal sex may indicate underlying intimacy issues for which help is necessary to overcome.

Sex with others

Christians have too often conformed themselves to the world's standards about sex, especially sex outside of marriage. This category includes casual sex ("hooking up"), friends-with-benefits, sex in dating relationships, cohabitation (living together), and affairs (adultery). Each of these involves two (or more) people in some relationship, although the relationship in hooking up is little more than a mutual agreement for sex. It differs from prostitution in the sense that, in theory, both parties are interested in sex for pleasure. Prostitutes sell themselves for financial purposes with little interest in the sex itself.

Each of these practices has crept into Christian circles. How we perceive the validity of them depends on how we see (1) God's design for marriage, (2) God's principles for sex outside of marriage, and (3) The seriousness of violating God's design, i.e., how we perceive the seriousness of sin.

In Chapter One, we saw as God's design for marriage: "For this reason a man shall leave his father and his mother, and be joined to his wife; and they shall become one flesh" (Gen. 2:24). God designed husband and wife to enjoy sex within marriage (Chapter One). Sex *outside* of wedlock is against God's design, that is, it is a sin. We must decide which view of sex is best: the world's view or God's view. We must also decide whether the message of the Bible (including "flee immorality") is actually good or whether the world and the flesh offer a better alternative. Of course, we know the "church answers," but each believer must decide whether he or she believes this to be true.

When we compare Scripture with these five categories of sex with others, we find that all of them violate the definition of purity: "*glorifying God by applying biblical principles regarding my sexual practices*" and several of the principles in the description of purity, especially that we make godly choices:

- by avoiding all inappropriate sexual activity
- that glorify God
- that honor others
- that I act on with my heart, mind, eyes, and actions

Of the five practices, three clearly violate God's design for sex and marriage either by cheapening sex ("hooking up" and friends-with-benefits) or by violating the marriage covenant (adultery). The friends-with-benefits option, while in the context of a relationship, sees sex as a mere expression of friendship or as a physical "need" and something we simply do. The book explored these ideas previously, and thus no more will be said here. The other two—sex in dating and cohabitation—deserve further comment.

Dating

Singles face the problem of dating in a sexually saturated culture. Our culture asks, "How long should we date before we have sex?" We know the answer *should* be "After we say 'I do,'" but culture gives a different answer. Just for fun, I went to the website "Ask.com" and asked the question, "How long should two people date before having sex?"[119] The results, while not statistically meaningful, are nevertheless intriguing. In one poll, half of the respondents said "six months or less." Over a quarter said "five dates or less." Comments abound like "Providing the two people having sex are mature adults there shouldn't be any problems because of it being too early" and "whenever the two people are comfortable with it." Some people in our culture still wish to wait until marriage, but, they belong to a minority. As the age gap grows between the onset of adolescence and saying "I do," the cultural message *seems* so much more sensible than the message to wait.

I am not going to pretend to understand the sexual pressures faced by singles today. I have been married for over 40 years, and haven't dated anyone other than my wife since my first year of college. I do, however, understand that the Bible says "Flee immorality," a command independent of a person's marital status and independent of cultural mores. I do understand that the Bible affirms God's faithfulness and promises He will provide a "way of escape." I know people who successfully waited until their wedding night. I even know one couple who waited until the marriage ceremony for their first kiss! They married after college and chose to wait until then to prevent starting their engines too soon. Consider these suggestions to help maintain purity while dating:

- Decide *before* dating that you want to remain chaste during the relationship.

- Do not date an unbeliever! This may sound old-fashioned or narrow, but none-the-less, it is sound. If you are a believer and she is not, the two of you built your relationship on two different worldviews. Dating and purity sometimes have difficulty mixing even when *both* of you are believers. You *cannot* reasonably expect an unbeliever to understand or accept biblical boundaries in relationships. I have heard both

---

119 www.ask.com, accessed June 3, 2016.

single men and single women say, "I cannot find any other believers to date!" But if God promised to meet our needs (and He has), we need to trust God to provide the right person in due time. The issue is a heart issue: Are we willing to wait on God and trust Him, or are we going to take things into our own hands?

- Early in the dating relationship, clearly define your boundaries. Keep in mind, men and women think differently, so explain that you set these limits to glorify God and to honor her. If either of you is unwilling to abide by the boundaries of the other, don't date!

- "Group date" frequently. We are less likely to misbehave in a group than when alone with our date. When you do date alone, avoid seclusion.

- Avoid being alone with her in a home, apartment, or motel room.

- Have personal conversations in semi-public places, such as a coffee shop. Such discussions in private may well lead to crossing boundaries.

- If either of you crosses a boundary, say "No!" out loud, and change your circumstances. For example, if you start "making out" in the parking lot, get out of the car or start the car and drive away.

Singles can—and should—spend time with the opposite sex. Just be careful to avoid dating according to cultural expectations!

Cohabitation

"Between 50 and 70 percent of couples today are thought to be cohabiting before marrying."[120] For many, this serves as a marriage substitute. What is the rationale for this living arrangement?

---

120 Regenerus and Uecker, 199.

- Some say they are evaluating whether they are compatible. However, this ignores the reality that overall compatibility—including sexual compatibility—develops over the course of a healthy marriage. Plus, several studies show that those who cohabitate and get married suffer a higher divorce rate than those who marry without first living together.[121] Plus, a high percentage of those who cohabitate split up, never marrying.[122]

- Some say they are afraid of marriage or that they have few positive role models of healthy marriages. Sadly, these reasons hold some validity. Many who survived broken homes fear their marriage will end in divorce as did their parent's marriage. They are (rightly) fearful. And the high rate of divorce combined with far too many anemic marriages does make it difficult to find positive role models. However, the Scriptures give the design for marriage, describe how to live as a believer ("walk by the Spirit"), and describe the faithfulness of God in our relationship with Him. The believer has the best model to follow. Will we allow the bad track record of marriage—even within Christian circles—to influence us towards cohabitation or will we follow God's standard?

- Some do so because culture, friends, or family encourage cohabitation as a valid and good relationship. However, such validation should not override God's design.

Cohabitation fails as a marriage substitute. The relationship requires no binding commitment to one another. "If the great theme of marriage

---

121 Ibid., 202; Linda J. Waite and Maggie Gallagher, *The Case for Marriage: Why Married People Are Happier, Healthier, and Better Off Financially* (New York, NY: Doubleday, 2000), 46.

122 One study reports that only one in five result in marriage (Robert Schoen, Nancy S. Landale, and Kimberly Daniels, "Family Transitions in Young Adulthood," *Demography* 44 [2007]: 807-200, in Regenerus and Uecker, 199).

is union, the counterriff [*sic*] of cohabitation is individualism . . . By consciously withholding permanent commitment, cohabitors do not reap the advantages of a deeper relationship."[123] The mentality of "if it doesn't work, we can always split up" fails to meet the "cleave" aspect of God's design. Although cohabitation requires more commitment than many relationships, such as friends-with-benefits, it does not fulfill the criteria of God's design. And since it is not a legitimate marriage substitute, it is a sinful lifestyle.

If you are not living with someone, do not start. If you are living with someone, start the process of moving out, and move out as quickly as possible. Or, you may choose to marry your partner, but move out as soon as possible and do not move back until *after* the wedding. If you do opt for marriage, I highly recommend premarital counseling.

The Bottom Line

Most circumstances from which we need to flee are variations of controlling our eyes and our thoughts. Some involve other women, but many circumstances require fleeing from sexual images or messages. The key to successful fleeing lies in understanding the faithfulness of God who promises to provide a way of escape and in the power of the Holy Spirit who promises we need not indulge the desires of the flesh. Fleeing unexpected sexual temptations becomes easier when we take care of our spiritual life and other areas of sexual temptation. We cannot eliminate every circumstance which may pass our way, but we can escape. We are commanded to flee, we are equipped to flee, and we must flee for the sake of our purity!

---

123 Waite and Gallagher, 44-45.

CHAPTER ELEVEN

MOVING AHEAD

My grandfather had a line that I loved: "Today is the tomorrow that was bugging us yesterday!" To experience purity over the long haul, we need to think about our "tomorrows" because they will soon become "today." I suspect you have questions about how to keep enjoying purity. So, in this chapter, I am going to ask, and briefly answer, some common issues that arise.

Q: What do I do to put things in place once I put the book down?

My favorite book is *Les Miserables*, written by Victor Hugo. I've seen the musical, I've seen the movie, and I read the unabridged version of the novel (all 1400 pages). I recently started rereading the book, and I was amazed at how much of the story I had forgotten over the years since I first read the book. Books are like that: After we finish reading them, the details, and maybe even some of the most important points, fade from memory. This book is no different. If all you do is read the book and then put it on the shelf, many of the principles we have discussed will fade from your memory. If your goal is limited to reading the book, this is not a problem. If your goal is to learn skills to better experience sexual purity, then forgetting the principles will certainly not help! I do not pretend to think that this book provides all the definitive answers for purity, but I do believe the principles are biblical, sound, and helpful. How do the principles become life-changers rather than faded memories? Let me offer six principles to help us move forward:

1. Write down whatever principles you learned that are helpful. Place this list of principles someplace so you can periodically review them.

2. Make a list of concrete actions you need to make to improve your purity. These measures could be things like canceling your pay movie channels on cable, installing a filter or reporting program on your computer, choosing to avoid R-rated movies and so on.

3. If you do not have an ME (accountability) partner, approach someone about starting an accountability relationship. If you have an ME partner, give him a copy of the two lists you made, and ask him to check on your progress periodically.

4. Make a list of verses that can encourage you, whether verses we discussed in this book or others. Memorize these verses and meditate on them periodically. The verses to start with should address the issues you first want to address in your life. For example, if you are concerned about eye control, memorize and meditate on a passage like Job 31:1; if you are worried about thought control, memorize and meditate on a passage like Philippians 4:8.

5. Be patient. Change usually takes time. Once in a while, Christians experience significant life changes quickly. Usually, however, such growth takes time! Allow time for growth; allow time to learn new skills; allow time to implement changes in your life. We may realize we need to work in many areas of our life, but we often discover we can only focus on one or two areas of change at a time. Choose

those that are the most important in your life, and work on those first.

6. Periodically, take the book off your shelf (this book or any other you found helpful) and reread or skim the book to encourage you in areas in which you are growing and to remind you of principles you may have forgotten.

Q: What if I slip?

Only knowing what purity is and *how* to experience it is not the same as *actually* experiencing it. What happens if, while pursuing purity in the big picture, at some point I choose to yield to sexual sin? I visit www.woo_hoo_hoo_xxx.com and masturbate to what I see. I feel guilty afterward, and I might even feel like a failure (shame).

I need to be careful in answering this question. Slips are not uncommon, but in no way do I wish to convey the idea that they are inevitable. Nor do I want to convey the idea that a slip is not a serious sin. However, because slips are possible, we need to address them. John, in his first epistle, dealt with this same tension:

> My little children, I am writing these things to you so that you may not sin. And if anyone sins, we have an Advocate with the Father, Jesus Christ the righteous (1 John 2:1)

"These things" look back to chapter one, where John encourages his readers to experience fellowship with God, who "is Light, and in Him there is no darkness at all." Notice the parallel between John and Isaiah? Isaiah saw his sinfulness because he saw the holiness of God; John addresses God's holiness (light) to motivate his readers not to sin.

Even though John wants his readers not to sin, he acknowledges that they will not experience a sinless life. He says *if* we say we are sinless, we deceive ourselves (1:8); *if* we say we have not sinned, we make Him a liar (1:10); and *if* anyone sins, we have an advocate (2:1). In the Greek, the structure of each of these statements represents a *probable future condition*, that is, it expresses something that will likely happen.[124] Because we are not yet perfect, we will sin from time to time.

John gives us the solution for these sins:

> If we confess our sins, He is faithful and righteous to forgive us our sins and to cleanse us from all unrighteousness. (1 John 1:9)

This verse addresses believers.[125] The consequence of our sin is a break in family fellowship with God, not the loss of salvation. When we confess our sin, we agree with God that what we did was, in fact, wrong. Confession means far more than saying something generic like, "forgive my sins." It is also different than "I am sorry I got caught." Instead, it means taking ownership for what we do and admitting the sin as sin. Confession of a sexual sin might sound like this:

> Father, I intentionally accessed an internet porn site. I chose to look at the images, and I decided to masturbate to those images. I chose to ignore your faithfulness, and so I did not look for the way of escape you promised. I chose to ignore the power of the Holy Spirit within me, and I sinned. Thank you for forgiving me.

Confession stops the process of distancing ourselves from God and turns us back in the right direction to restore intimacy with Him.

But wait. Some may ask, "If I am a Christian, aren't all of my sins already forgiven?" Passages like Ephesians 1:7 and Colossians 2:13 make it clear that we have been forgiven *all* our trespasses. But the forgiveness John speaks about is different than the forgiveness in these two passages. Forgiveness in the Ephesians and Colossians passages deals with our *positional* standing before God, our "in Christ" position. John, however, deals with our family relationship with God, not our position:

---

124 Ray Summers, *Essentials of New Testament Greek*, (Nashville, TN: Broadman & Holman Publishers, 1995), 121.

125 Notice how often the words *we*, *us*, and *our* appear in I John 1:6-2:2!

Although we are seated with Christ as fully accepted and forgiven people, we live down here on earth, and our ongoing sins must receive the forgiveness of our heavenly Father if we are to be in fellowship with Him. This is not hard to understand, since earthly parent/child relationships work exactly the same way. If a child has never told a parent 'I am sorry,' something is clearly wrong in the relationship, even though the child remains his parent's child. In the same way, as born again people, we are permanently in the family of God; but when harmony with our Father is breached, He requires confession as the condition for restoring that harmony.[126]

We need to address four issues related to this confession. The first is *guilt*. When I sin, I should feel guilt, a legitimate response since I did something wrong: I have sinned, I have acted contrary to God's will and contrary to who I am as a believer. When I confess my sins, this guilt is dealt with since God forgave the sin (the emotions may linger). However, I might still *feel* guilty. But this feeling is false guilt—I feel guilty although God's Word promises He forgave me. The cure for this false guilt is meditation on the promise of forgiveness in 1 John 1:9, allowing the truth of Scripture to correct the error in our thinking.

The second issue deals with the slip itself. I use the word *slip* because the choices to yield to temptation represent deviations from the overall lifestyle of purity I am striving to live. The word "slip" does not minimize the sinfulness of the choice, and it does not mean we will experience no consequences. Will we deal with the sin and return to practicing purity or will we allow the slip to drive us back to a lifestyle earmarked by impurity? After we've taken the corrective step of confessing our sin to God, start moving forward again. Start enjoying purity again. Don't minimize the failure, but don't let it kick you off the right path, either.

---

126 Zane C. Hodges, *The Epistles of John: Walking in the Light of God's Love* (Irving, TX: Grace Evangelical Society, 1999), 67.

When we slip, we need to practice three simple steps. First, confess the sin to God (1 John 1:9) as discussed above. Second, call your ME (Mutual Encouragement) partner and tell him about the incident without making excuses. Third, address your thoughts so that you can begin experiencing purity again immediately. After slipping, we commonly condemn ourselves in our thoughts, or we contemplate giving up. Both can lead to long-term failure.

That leads to the third issue: The difference between fail*ing* and being a fail*ure*. When we slip, we've committed serious sin. We did not succeed in practicing purity, we failed to apply the provisions God provides us for life, we failed to obey God. When we act out, we are *failing* in sexual purity. Failing is serious, but that does not mean I am a fail*ure*. Fail*ing* is a guilt issue; seeing ourselves as a fail*ure* is a shame issue (Chapter Five). Too often, we let our thinking take us down the wrong path from guilt to shame. We believe the lie that it is impossible to experience purity because of some inherent flaw within us. We believe the lie instead of the promises of God that we can walk in purity by His power.

As a fourth and final issue, we must recognize whether we are occasionally failing or whether we are failing as a pattern. Neither says anything about our salvation.[127] We cannot objectively define how frequently we must sin for it to be habitual, but I think most of us we can subjectively identify when we are stuck in a pattern. We just "know." Being stuck should drive us back to the beginning of the process and rethinking key ideas:

- Check our motives: Do we want purity in our life, or are we simply saying we do because we know that is the "right" answer?

- Do we have the right goals for our purity, or have we set our goals too low?

---

127 Unfortunately, some hold the view that "habitual" sin implies we either lost our salvation or we were never really saved. I believe differently; that our salvation is secured and assured by the work of the Trinity on our behalf. No sin, no matter how habitual, implies we are not saved. See Anderson, *Position And Condition*.

- Have we worked through the process and identified the sources of temptation that most often trip us up?

- Are we working at eye control and thought control?

- Are we trusting the Holy Spirit to empower us as we practice the principles of purity?

- Are we still on the steep part of the learning curve? New skills take time to master. In the initial phases of learning, applying them feels awkward, and we sense failure more frequently. Are we still in that phase where we are learning how to apply the principles?

If the answer to most of these questions is "yes," we may need help from a pastor or counselor in discovering the underlying issues in our lives that trip us up. Seeking this help is not a sign of weakness, in fact, it is just the opposite. It recognizes we need some outside, objective help to discover issues that cause us problems.

If the answer to any specific questions is "yes," then go back to the section of the book that addresses the issue. What do you need to rethink about that area of your life? What do you need to do differently? Do you just need to give yourself time to master the skill?

So, slips are not inevitable, but they are likely. They are sinful, and we must deal with them as sin, but they do not mean we have failed entirely. If we slip, confess the sin and begin again. Press forward!

Q: What if I am not experiencing intimacy with my wife?

Keep in mind my purity cannot depend on my relationship with my wife. God did design us to enjoy sex within marriage, but I am responsible for my purity *regardless* of our sex life. To improve intimacy with our brides, we might need to rethink our view of intimacy (see Chapter Two). We need to work on understanding our wives. Addressing marriage and marital intimacy is really beyond the scope of this work, but I do want to prompt you towards working on your relationship with your spouse. Many good resources and conferences are available which can help with this.[128] Talk to your pastor to help identify specific resources. Work on intimacy because it is the right thing to do, not because you only want more (or better) sex. In that case, once your wife realizes that sex is your only real goal, she may well feel used, hurt, and angry. Neither true intimacy nor sexual intimacy will improve.

Q: What do I do if the internal temptation doesn't wane?

Once in a while (maybe more often for some of us) it seems the internal temptation just won't die. We try to apply everything we know how to do, but the yearnings just don't go away. I meditate on Scripture to change my thinking, but my thoughts snap back to the temptation. I try to visualize my favorite fishing hole, but my mind snaps back to the sexual images in my mind. You get the idea. You likely have experienced this!

What do we do if we still face a seemingly unrelenting temptation? We have only three options: (1) Give in, and hope that the pressure decreases (not a good choice, by the way); (2) "White knuckle" it and just hang on (which may work for awhile, but rarely brings long-term success) or, (3) Believe what the Bible says about God and what He has provided for us. Remember this?

---

128 Family Life Ministries provides many good resources, including books and marriage conferences (www.familylife.com). Some excellent books you may wish to work through as a couple include Dr. Emerson Eggeriches, *Love and Respect: The Love She Most Desires; The Respect He Desperately Needs,* (Nashville, TN: Thomas Nelson, 2004) or the pair of books, *For Men Only* and *For Women Only.* The authors of these two books suggest each partner first read the book about them (i.e., men read *For Women Only*), highlighting points that are true of them, then swapping books. That way, when the husband reads the book about women, she will have helped him see what points are important to her and *vice versa.* (Shaunti Feldhahn and Jeff Feldhahn, *For Men Only: A, Straightforward Guide to the Inner Lives of Women* rev. ed., [Colorado Springs, CO: Multnomah Books, 2006, 2013], Shaunti Feldhahn, *For Women Only: What You Need to Know about the Inner Lives of Men,* rev. ed., [Colorado Springs, CO: Multnomah Books, 2004, 2013]).

No temptation has overtaken you but such as is common to man; and God is faithful, who will not allow you to be tempted beyond what you are able, but with the temptation will provide the way of escape also, so that you will be able to endure it. 1 Corinthians 10:13

God's character (faithfulness) and His promise to provide a way of escape provide the keys to enduring temptation. The verse says nothing about how *long* we may need to face it! So, if this verse is true—and it is—then the problem with seemingly unrelenting temptation is discovering different "ways of escape." They exist—we just need to find them! Here is the heart of the solution: *Read the Bible and pray.*

I can hear the groans now. "Of course, I should read and pray—isn't that the 'standard' Christian answer?" Yes, but this is not a trite, generic answer. Read and pray *with purpose*! Read slowly through the Psalms (remember the exercise in Chapter Five?). As you read, take notes. When you pray:

1. Tell God you are struggling and want to endure the temptations successfully

2. Ask Him to reveal anything in your life that may be driving the temptation

3. Ask God to protect you if some external source (such as Satan and his forces) are fueling the temptations

4. Give particular thanks for the characteristics of God you rediscovered in the Psalms.

Your prayer could sound something like this:

Father, you know the temptation I am battling right now. You know I cannot seem to shake it, but you also know I want to endure it successfully. I know you have promised a way of escape, so please help me discover what you have provided. If it is something I am doing or not doing, reveal that to me as well. If the source is something Satan and his forces are throwing my way, please protect me from them. I read today in the Psalms that "in You, I have taken my refuge." You are my refuge, and I thank you that in you I am safe. Thank you for being such a good God.

Don't expect immediate relief. It may come immediately, but trusting God means we trust Him no matter how long we must wait for resolution. Do not give up!!

Q: What do I do if my accountability (ME) partner is inadequate to help?

Accountability often comes with issues. It only helps to the degree that I am honest with my ME friend. But the effectiveness of accountability may also be limited by my partner's limitations. A pastor from the West Coast recently told me "accountability in the area of sexual purity doesn't work. Too many accountability partners aren't equipped to help. The answers they give are too simple. And the younger generation doesn't like accountability." His statements are mostly true, but they are not universal.

Keep in mind that ME is but one piece of the process towards purity and that no ME relationship is perfect. Here are some questions to help improve this relationship:

- Are you honest with your partner?

- Is your partner someone who is willing to ask you the hard questions or does he tend to downplay your actions when you tell him about them? If he is not willing to ask the hard questions, you may need to find someone else to serve as an ME friend.

- Do you discuss more than just sexual issues? Most ME relationships function more efficiently when they look at all of life, not just sexual purity.

- Is your partner equipped to help you with your struggles? Sometimes, once we become transparent with one another, we discover that the issues are more complex or profound than he can handle. In this situation, seek help from someone with the skill set you need, such as a counselor or pastor. Don't give up on your ME friend, but don't be afraid to seek the additional help you need! Your partner can encourage you to follow up on any appointments you make with someone.

Q: I have a strong sex drive—am I a sex addict?

Addiction has nothing to do with the strength of our sex drive. Some men have more powerful drives than others. Patrick Carnes, a secular expert on sexual addiction, differentiates between sex drive and addiction this way:

> The notion of sexual addiction is sometimes confused with a positive, pleasurable, and intense sexuality enjoyed by a 'normal' population. It is sometimes confused with simply enjoying frequent sex—what's 'frequent' to some is the norm for others. Also, many people experience what they would term sexual excess. But, they learn to moderate their behavior. They are able to stop and say no. Sex addicts have lost control over their ability to say no; they have lost control over their ability to choose.[129]

Elsewhere, Carnes describes a variety of sexual behaviors and concludes, "Engaging in behaviors that fit within a specific behavior type does not necessarily make a person a sex addict. The pattern of loss of control does."[130] In other words, it is not the frequency of sexual interest, the intensity of the sexual drive, or the type of sexual activities a man pursues that define addiction. So, no, a strong sex drive does not necessarily—or even probably—imply sexual addiction.

---

129 Patrick Carnes, Ph.D., *Contrary to Love: Helping the Sexual Addict* (Center City, MN: Hazelden Educational Materials, 1989), 4-5.

130 Carnes, *Don't Call It Love: Recovery From Sexual Addiction* (New York: Bantam Books, 1992), 44.

Given the simplified definition of sexual addiction as a sin or sickness "involving any type of *uncontrollable* sexual activity,"[131] about ten percent of the men who took my survey said they were "probably addicted." A much higher percentage of single men (25%) and men inactive in their faith (23%) reported they were probably addicted.

> Contrary to enjoying sex as a self-affirming source of physical pleasure, the sex addict has learned to rely on sex for comfort from pain, nurturing, or relief from stress . . . Contrary to love, the obsessional illness transforms sex into the primary relationship or need, for which all else may be sacrificed, including family, friends, values, health, safety, and work.[132]

Sexual addiction is as real and as powerful as substance addiction, and not easy to overcome alone.

Addiction is not "just" a disease; it starts with of a pattern of sinful choices. Being addicted does not give permission to justify sexual sin ("I couldn't help myself—I'm addicted"). Addiction does add additional layers of issues which the person must deal with in addition to the typical storms of temptation. The addict may need to address personal issues from his past. Often, his life history includes sexual, emotional, or physical abuse. His home may have been highly dysfunctional. And sometimes, someone develops an addiction simply because of easy access to sexual material combined with a distorted view of sex. Thus, addicts face all the same temptations as other men but must deal with the additional effects of the addiction.

Keep in mind, the addict's loss of control over his ability to choose is neither absolute nor permanent. It does not mean he has no ability whatsoever; it means he has deeply ingrained patterns that are difficult to overcome. His thinking and practices may have altered his brain chemistry. Thus, an addict can say no (he is not helpless), but the *compulsion* to act is so strong it *feels* impossible to do so. As a

---

131 Mark Laaser, *Faithful & True: Sexual Integrity in a Fallen World* (Grand Rapids, MI: Zondervan Publishing House, 1996), 21.

132 Carnes, *Contrary to Love*, 5.

result, his lifestyle reflects an overall inability to say no. Because of the added complexities unique to addiction, it is much harder for an addict to make right choices than for a non-addict making those same choices.

The tools in this book can help the addict, but he probably needs more help than this book can provide. If that is you, take advantage of the good resources that are available to help with sexual addiction in conjunction with counseling help.[133] Recovery groups such as Celebrate Recovery* provide support for many men.[134] Someone addicted to sex should not try to overcome the addiction in isolation; rarely (if ever) do such efforts bring long-term success! Addiction is not easy to overcome, but the power of the Holy Spirit is greater than the power of the addiction. There is help and hope for overcoming sexual addiction.

Q: What if I didn't see anything in this book about my specific temptation?

I have mentioned many temptations that are common to men. In fact, many that I mentioned were identified as sources of them by men who completed my survey. My intent is not to list every possible temptation men face. The scope of what tempts men sexually is too vast to explore every option. The fact that this book does not mention a specific temptation says nothing about the seriousness of that temptation. I did not write about "acceptable" temptations and skip "twisted" ones. Every kind of sexual sin is a problem, and the principles outlined in the book apply no matter what issues we face. Even if you don't see the temptation with which you struggle, the character of God and the character of the promises of Scripture hold. They are unconditional, regardless of the particular issue.

---

133 I would recommend Russell Willingham, *Breaking Free: Understanding Sexual Addiction & the Healing Power of Jesus* (Downers Grove, IL: InterVarsity Press, 1999) or Mark Laaser, *Healing the Wounds of Sexual Addiction* (Grand Rapids, MI: Zondervan Publishing House, 2004). Laaser has other resources available through his website, www.faithfulandtrue.com.

134 www.celebraterecovery.com

Q: What do I do if I feel I am failing at controlling my eyes or thoughts?

"Nice try, Roger. Your theories sound good. But you know what? When I'm at the mall, a cute young thing walks by, my radar eyes lock on, my head turns, and I watch, well, you know what I'm watching! I'm a guy, and I can't help that I'm visual. The world I live in entices me in more ways than you can imagine. Men cannot control their eyes and thoughts—it runs counter to our world and our makeup!"

Sound familiar? Part of the argument is correct: Just like this objector, I am a guy; I am visual, and the world I live in entices me in many ways. But one key phrase is wrong! Men *can* control their eyes and thoughts! How do I know? Because if the flesh wins and cannot lose, then the promise of Scripture is false. Remember the words, "walk by the Spirit, and you will not carry out the desire of the flesh"? If I *necessarily* carry out the desires of the flesh (i.e., I cannot help it, ever), then this statement in the Word of God is a lie. Strong words, but true. Either the Scriptures are true, or they are not. I believe they are true!

So, what *do* I do if I feel I am failing at controlling my eyes or my thoughts? This is a common question. As discussed earlier in the chapter, learning something new almost always takes time to master. Eventually, we become good at applying what we've learned, but before that point, we struggle with the learning curve. We feel like we fail more than we succeed. If you feel like you are failing at controlling your eyes or controlling your thoughts, don't give up. Keep practicing. With practice and time, we can succeed more than we do not manage. Think long range: If you need to struggle for several months before you feel like you are winning more often than losing, going through the struggle is worth it! You stand to gain a lifetime of control. Give yourself enough time for the skill to become easier.

But there may be another reason we are failing. If we are not diligent; if we are inconsistent in practicing the skills, we cannot expect success. The problem is not with God, or with His Word or His power. The problem is us! We cannot expect life change connected with sexual purity or any other area of life by applying the principles half-heartedly. Ask yourself the question (and answer *honestly*): Do I want to control my eyes and thoughts or do I prefer to enjoy the images and thoughts that come my way?

Q: How long do I have to work on purity? When will I have this mastered?

My home in Texas sat on a three-quarter acre lot. One Sunday afternoon, I put on my headphones, tuned into the Houston Astros baseball game on the radio, jumped on my riding mower, and mowed the lot. I finished the mowing and, before jumping in the shower to get rid of the sweat, grime, and grass, I admired my handiwork. The lawn looked good! After the shower, I called the local paper and placed an ad to sell the mower. After all, the lawn did look good, so I had it mastered, right? Never needed mowing again.

Wrong!

Left to itself, the appearance of the yard deteriorates. It takes constant care to keep it looking nice.

Our sexual purity acts the same way. The default position is conformity to the world. Transformation takes on-going renewal and practice!

Remember Paul's admonition, "Therefore let him who thinks he stands take heed that he does not fall"? Enjoying sexual purity takes diligence. It's a life-long practice. It becomes easier over time, but if we think we have "made it," we set ourselves up for failure. Jesus said discipleship requires taking up our cross "daily" (Luke 9:23): it is a life-long practice. That's why it takes more than reading a book to experience purity; it requires daily practices which change us over a lifetime.

EPILOGUE

The End—and the Beginning!

And so we come to the end of the book. My prayer is that this is just the beginning of a lifetime of enjoying purity, a purity that is far more than just avoiding certain activities. In Chapter two, we defined purity as *Glorifying God by applying biblical principles regarding my sexual practices*, and described it this way:

I experience purity to the degree that I make godly choices

- *by avoiding all inappropriate sexual activity*
- *by enjoying appropriate expressions of masculinity*
- *by enjoying appropriate relations with the opposite sex*
- *that glorify God*
- *that respect myself*
- *that honor others*
- *that I act on with my heart, mind, eyes, and actions.*

My prayer is that we—you and I—will enjoy a lifetime of glorifying God with our sexual purity. If you found any principles or hints helpful, use them! If you pick up useful points from other resources, use them as well. Use whatever tools help you learn the commands and principles of God as revealed in the Word of God and apply them in your life by the power of the Holy Spirit of God for the glory of God. To the degree this work moves you in that direction, I give thanks to God.

Let's briefly review the key points. Experiencing purity begins by building on a strong foundation—the person, power, and provisions of God. The indwelling Holy Spirit gives us the ability to change. When we walk by the Spirit (hearing the Word with faith, then in faith responding to Him) we can successfully say "no" to the flesh and say "yes" to God. One key promise He gives is 1 Corinthians 10:13:

> No temptation has overtaken you but such as is common to man; and God is faithful, who will not allow you to be tempted beyond what you are able, but with the temptation will provide the way of escape also, so that you will be able to endure it.

Our faithful God promises a "way of escape" whenever we face a temptation.

We described five fundamental principles which form the frame of the house (our purity) we build on the foundation. The first principle (*connect regularly with God*) addresses our day-to-day relationship with God. The second principle (*involve others*) addresses the need to allow other people to help us in our walk. God did not design us to live the Christian life in solitude. Purity, which is one dimension of our Christian life, is no different. The third principle (*control your thoughts*) addresses how we can control what we are thinking. The key is not to stop a thought pattern; rather, it is to *change* what we are thinking. We can turn our thoughts to Scriptures or other positive memories (like a golf game or fishing trip). The key here is thinking about God, His Word, or His good gifts instead of dwelling on unhealthy sexual thoughts. The fourth principle (*control your eyes*) teaches us to redirect our eyes from whatever sexual image caught our attention to something neutral or positive. And the fifth principle (*flee!*) teaches us to flee any temptation that pops up.

We have reached the end of the book. But my prayer is, we are at the beginning of a long walk enjoying sexual purity for our good and His glory. Press on. See what God does in your life. Enjoy life as a stormproof man!

SCRIPTURE INDEX